Challenge Your Mind
Word Games
Throughout the Year

Cover Illustration
by
Vickie Lane

Inside Art
by
Randy Rider

Publishers
Instructional Fair • TS Denison
Grand Rapids, Michigan 49544

Permission to Reproduce

Credits

Authors: Jan Kennedy, Wendy Roh Jenks, Jodi Fair
Cover Artist: Vickie Lane
Inside Illustrations: Randy Rider
Project Director/Editor: Linda Kimble
Editors: Elizabeth Flikkema, Linda Triemstra
Typesetting/Layout: Pat Geasler

About the Authors

Master teachers Jan Kennedy, Wendy Roh Jenks, and Jodi Fair contributed pages for this book. These educators have numerous years of elementary teaching experience and enjoyed the challenge of creating these pages. It is their hope that the children in your classrooms enjoy these brain ticklers.

Standard Book Number: 1-56822-664-0
Challenge Your Mind
Copyright © 1998 by Instructional Fair • TS Denison
2400 Turner Avenue NW
Grand Rapids, Michigan 49544

Table of Contents

Happy New Year!

Name _____

New Year's Day

January 1st is a new year with new challenges. Try this challenge by completing each word that contains "new." The definitions will help you.

1. The youngest infant   NEW __ ☐ __ __

2. Second part of the Christian Bible   NEW __ __ __ ☐ __ __ __ __ __

3. Neighbor of Vermont   NEW __ __ __ __ __ __ __ __

4. Broadcaster of the news   NEW __ __ __ __ __ __ __

5. Recently married   NEW __ __ __ __ __

6. Children's literature award   NEW __ __ __ __ __ __ __ __ __

7. Louisiana Mardi Gras city   NEW __ ☐ __ __ __ __

8. American actor   __ __ __ ☐ NEW __ __ __

9. Fruit-filled cookie   NEW __ ☐ __

10. Trenton is this state's capital   NEW __ __ __ __ __ __

11. A phase of the earth's satellite NEW __ __ __ ☐

12. A small salamander   NEW __

13. He discovered that gravity   ☐ __ __ __ __ __ __ __ NEW __ __ __
    held the universe together

14. A Canadian province   NEW __ __ ☐ __ __ __ __ __

15. A short movie of current events NEW __ __ __ __ __

16. One of the Four Corners states   NEW __ __ __ ☐ __ __

17. *U.S.A. Today*, *The Chicago Tribune*, etc.   NEW __ __ __ __ __ __

18. The Big Apple   NEW __ __ __ __

19. January holiday   NEW __ ☐ __ __ , __ __ __

List the letters from the boxes above. _____

Unscramble to form a word of promise for the New Year.

_____

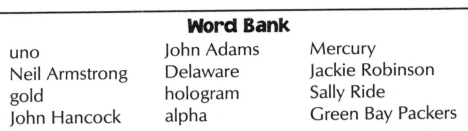

Famous Firsts

name _____

New Year's Day

Celebrate the first day of the new year by researching these famous first facts. Match each word from the Word Bank to its definition. The letter boxes may help you do this more easily.

Word Bank

uno	John Adams	Mercury
Neil Armstrong	Delaware	Jackie Robinson
gold	hologram	Sally Ride
John Hancock	alpha	Green Bay Packers

1. first signer of the Declaration of Independence

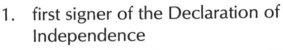

2. first state to ratify the constitution

3. number one in Spanish

4. first planet from the sun

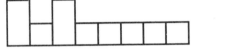

5. first president to live in the White House

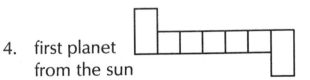

6. first discovered in California on January 24, 1848

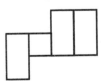

7. first black major-league baseball player

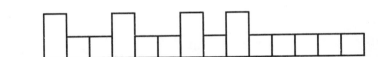

8. winners of the first Super Bowl

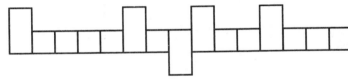

9. first man on the moon

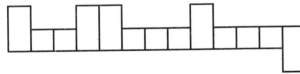

10. Dennis Gabor was first to invent this.

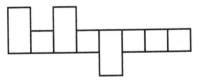

11. first female American astronaut in space

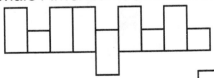

12. first letter of the Greek alphabet

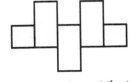

 5

IF8727 Challenge Your Mind

Cheer the New Year!

Name _____

New Year's Day

Create a crazy story! Fold this page on the dotted line. While the right side is out of sight, write words in the blanks on the left. Then unfold the page and place your words in the story. Read it to a friend.

1. _____ classmate
2. _____ adjective (superlative)
3. _____ number
4. _____ famous person
5. _____ plural noun
6. _____ plural noun
7. _____ verb (past tense)
8. _____ adjective
9. _____ adjective
10. _____ verb (past tense)
11. _____ verb (past tense)
12. _____ noun
13. _____ noun
14. _____ verb (past tense)
15. _____ adjective

My friend _____ and I decided to have the
1
_____ New Year's party ever! We invited _____
2   3
of our classmates, and one celebrity, _____ . We
4
decorated the family room with _____ and
5
_____ . Our special celebrity guest _____ when
6   7
he/she saw how cool this party was going to be. We
played _____ music and danced crazy dances. We
8
snacked on _____ pizza, chips, and pop.
9

For a special treat, the celebrity _____ and
10
_____ . We were thrilled!
11

As the midnight hour grew closer, we sat in front of
the big screen _____ and watched the giant
12
_____ slowly descend in New York City. At 12:00,
13
we _____ and wished each other a very _____
14   15
New Year!

THE ROSE BOWL IS PLAYED ON NEW YEAR'S DAY IN PASADENA, CALIFORNIA! HUT-HUT!!

© Instructional Fair • TS Denison   IF8727 Challenge Your Mind

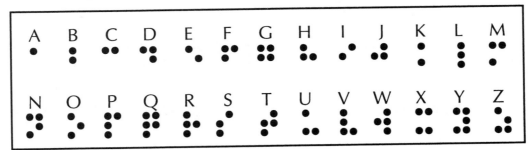

Braille Busters

name _____

Louis Braille's Birthday

Louis Braille was born on January 4, 1809. His invention of the Braille alphabet made it possible for blind people to read and write. Use the Braille alphabet below to decode these wintry riddles.

A	B	C	D	E	F	G	H	I	J	K	L	M
N	O	P	Q	R	S	T	U	V	W	X	Y	Z

1. What is the jelly jar's favorite month?

_____

2. What is Adam's favorite holiday?

_____

3. What do Eskimos use to stick things together?

_____

4. How do you eat evergreen ice cream?

_____

5. What is a liar's favorite month?

_____

6. What heavy snowstorm blanketed Emerald City?

_____

7. What do you get when your bike freezes?

An _____

8. What do Eskimos eat for breakfast?

_____

© Instructional Fair • TS Denison

IF8727 *Challenge Your Mind*

Holiday Happenings

Name _____

Year of Holidays

Find the holidays on the list above the wordsearch. Then write the holidays on the lines below in the order they occur throughout the year.

St. Patrick's Day	Thanksgiving	Independence Day	April Fools' Day
Columbus Day	Memorial Day	Martin L. King Day	Mother's Day
Christmas	Hanukkah	Father's Day	Valentine's Day
Labor Day	New Year's Day	Groundhog Day	Halloween

S	M	S	I	Y	A	D	S	R	E	H	T	O	M	T	D	Y	M
V	T	H	A	N	K	S	G	I	V	I	N	G	L	E	A	A	E
A	M	P	H	A	L	L	O	W	E	E	N	R	Y	Y	Y	D	M
L	E	M	A	R	T	I	N	L	K	I	N	G	D	A	Y	E	O
E	M	X	N	T	D	F	B	L	O	I	V	X	B	D	A	C	R
N	O	J	U	E	R	A	U	G	H	N	F	L	Y	G	D	N	I
T	T	I	K	M	S	I	V	X	B	O	R	A	S	O	S	E	A
I	F	M	K	N	E	K	C	P	Q	L	M	B	O	H	R	D	L
N	F	P	A	H	D	R	Y	K	I	D	J	O	T	D	A	N	D
E	B	A	H	I	Q	W	E	E	S	O	P	R	I	N	E	E	A
S	A	M	T	S	I	R	H	C	V	D	N	D	B	U	Y	P	Y
D	F	A	T	H	E	R	S	D	A	Y	A	A	S	O	W	E	B
A	P	R	I	L	F	O	O	L	S	D	A	Y	V	R	E	D	C
Y	L	D	F	T	N	O	R	A	B	D	T	A	S	G	N	N	I
S	T	E	E	W	Y	A	D	S	U	B	M	U	L	O	C	I	K

1. _____
2. _____
3. _____
4. _____
5. _____
6. _____
7. _____
8. _____
9. _____
10. _____
11. _____
12. _____
13. _____
14. _____
15. _____
16. _____

Duck, Duck . . .

name _____

French poet Charles Perrault is best remembered for his *Tales from Mother Goose*. Unscramble the letters to make words that describe these well-known Mother Goose and other story time characters. Write each word.

_____ Humpty Dumpty
M J P U Y

_____ Goldilocks
D L N E O G

_____ Ramona
R E B A V

_____ Rabbit
T E V E V E N L E

_____ Dog
S N I D G I G E T G

_____ Leo, the Lop
O A E L B V L

_____ Alexander
R G Y N A

_____ Snoopy
I S F N N F I G

_____ Crocodile
N U O O M S E R

"TALES FROM MOTHER GOOSE" WAS FIRST PUBLISHED IN 1697! IT INCLUDED CINDERELLA, SLEEPING BEAUTY AND RED RIDING HOOD!

Hail To the Chiefs

Name _____

Inauguration
Day—Jan. 20

The squares below contain parts of 18 presidents' names. Match the parts
and write the presidents' names on the lines. Cross off the squares as you use them.

velt	Jeff	ter	on	Lin	rd
hower	Mad	I	edy	Eisen	Gar
Kenn	Ad	erson	ison	do	Roose
Fo	solemnly	ington	coln	ton	field
land	Ta	Nix	nt	Buren	Cool
Clin	Wash	swear	Bu	Car	idge
Cleve	ft	Van	Gra	ams	sh

THE FIRST
INAUGURATION
OF A U.S.
PRESIDENT
TOOK PLACE
IN NEW
YORK CITY!

_____   _____   _____
_____   _____   _____
_____   _____   _____
_____   _____   _____
_____   _____   _____
_____

The remaining squares answer this question: *What are the first four words of the*

presidential oath? _____

© Instructional Fair • TS Denison

10

IF8727 *Challenge Your Mind*

Winter Wordsearch

name _____

Winter Weather

It's a winter wonderland of words. Figure out what words fit the definitions below, then circle the words in the wordsearch. (↑ ↓ → ← ↙ ↘)

A	F	P	S	E	K	A	L	F	W	O	N	S	T	S
T	V	Q	P	O	E	S	H	O	V	E	L	N	E	N
E	I	A	O	C	I	T	C	R	A	E	I	O	L	O
M	C	B	L	I	Z	Z	A	R	D	L	R	W	A	W
P	E	B	A	A	D	R	S	K	I	F	O	B	C	M
E	C	M	R	I	N	O	O	J	G	R	T	L	I	O
R	A	P	B	D	I	C	I	C	L	E	C	O	T	B
A	S	F	E	E	N	O	H	S	O	E	A	W	C	I
T	T	G	A	N	J	C	K	E	O	Z	F	E	R	L
U	L	F	R	I	G	I	D	T	D	I	L	R	A	E
R	E	V	N	Q	L	U	V	R	I	N	L	V	T	O
E	S	W	S	L	I	D	I	N	G	G	I	W	N	N
X	Y	T	S	O	R	F	U	N	T	S	H	J	A	S
K	C	S	L	A	T	S	Y	R	C	W	C	X	O	M

Bonus Box

Try to find these words in the wordsearch too:

frost

snowblower

chill factor

crystals

frigid

freezing

sliding

Arctic

snowmobile

ice castles

1. a spike of ice __ __ __ __ __ __

2. a large mass of snow sliding down a mountain slope
__ __ __ __ __ __ __ __ __

3. a heavy and windy snowstorm
__ __ __ __ __ __ __ __

4. measure of warm or cold
__ __ __ __ __ __ __ __ __ __ __

5. a heap of snow
__ __ __ __ __

6. a bird that can't fly
__ __ __ __ __ __ __

7. a house built with blocks of hard snow __ __ __ __ __

8. small crystals of snow
__ __ __ __ __ __ __ __ __ __

9. large white animal of the Arctic
__ __ __ __ __ __ __ __

10. a scoop attached to a handle
__ __ __ __ __ __

11. used for sliding __ __ __ __

12. continent surrounding the South Pole
__ __ __ __ __ __ __ __ __ __

Hot off the Press!

name _____

These holiday books sound too good to miss! But you probably won't find them in your school library. See if you can match each book title to its author. The first one is done for you.

Book	Author
A. *The Littlest Angel*	1. __D__ Holly Berry
B. *New Orleans Magic*	2. ____ Barb E. Q.
C. *Did the Groundhog See His Shadow?*	3. ____ Howard I. No
D. *Decorating Tips for Christmas*	4. ____ Spar Klurs
E. *Crumbly Recipes for Thanksgiving*	5. ____ Mark Downs
F. *4th of July Is a Blast*	6. ____ Trot Err
G. *The Voyages of Columbus*	7. ____ Q. T. Pye
H. *Grilling Out on Labor Day*	8. ____ L. F. 8. Terr
I. *The Nutcracker Ballet Book*	9. ____ Marty Grah
J. *Kentucky Derby Losers*	10. ____ Dan D. Lions
K. *After-Christmas Sales*	11. ____ Minnie Hey Lo
L. *The New Year's Baby Book*	12. ____ Seamor Shamrocks
M. *St. Patrick's Field of Clover*	13. ____ I. C. A. Fleet
N. *Counting the Days 'Til Christmas*	14. ____ Dan Sir
O. *April Showers Bring May Weeds*	15. ____ Betty Cracker
P. *My Valentine Love*	16. ____ Hy I. Q.
Q. *Smart Kid's Guide to Holidays*	17. ____ Cal Q. Later
R. *The Ups and Downs of Holidays*	18. ____ Art Throb

"A VISIT FROM ST. NICHOLAS", THE FAMOUS POEM BY CLEMENT C. MOORE, WAS FIRST PUBLISHED IN 1822!

Famous Black Americans

name _____

In 1976, our country began honoring the contributions of Black Americans in the month of February.

Use the clues to fill in the crossword puzzle with the names of famous Black Americans.

DON'T FORGET JOEL CHANDLER HARRIS!

Across

1. A writer and poet, she was chosen by President Clinton to recite his inaugural poem.

2. Active in the Civil Rights Movement, she refused to give up her bus seat.

3. The first internationally famous trumpet soloist in American jazz. Louis _____

4. A former slave who made more than 300 products from peanuts.

5. The first black to win the Wimbleton Tennis Tournament, he also worked to fight AIDS.

Down:

1. She was the first black to sing with the Metropolitan Opera Company in New York City.

2. The first black professional baseball player.

3. He led the Civil Rights march on Washington.

4. She helped hundreds of slaves escape to freedom on the Underground Railroad.

5. He hit 725 home runs to top Babe Ruth's lifetime record of 714.

Famous Duos

Name _____

Use the letters on the phone pad to dial these famous pairs.

Example: DIAL = 2 3 1 4

A B C **1**	D E F **2**	G H I **3**
J K L **4**	M N O **5**	P Q R **6**
S T U **7**	V W X **8**	Y Z **9**

MY FAVORITE DUO IS BACON & EGGS!

1. 1 1 7 5 1 5   and   6 5 1 3 5   _____

2. 3 1 5 7 2 4   and   3 6 2 7 2 4   _____

3. 4 1 1 4   and   4 3 4 4   _____

4. 4 7 1 9   and   2 2 7 3   _____

5. 4 2 6 5 3 7   and   5 3 7 7   6 3 3 3 9   _____

6. 1 2 1 7 7 9   and the   1 2 1 7 7   _____

7. 1 1 4 8 3 5   and   3 5 1 1 2 7   _____

8. 5 3 5 5 3 2   and   5 3 1 4 2 9   5 5 7 7 2   _____

9. 4 1 2 9   and the   7 6 1 5 6   _____

10. 7 5 5 5 6 9   and   1 3 1 6 4 3 2   1 6 5 8 5   _____

Bee My Valentine

Name _____

Valentine's Day

Cross out the homonym in each valentine that is used incorrectly. Then write the correct spelling beside the heart.

Roses are read, violets are blue

My cup of tee

To sweet four me

Maid for me!

Too dad with love

Loves me knot

For my deer friend

Wood you be mine?

My heart beets for you.

Bee mine.

The won for me!

Eye only have eyes for you.

I'm crazy about ewe.

IF8727 *Challenge Your Mind*

Heart to Heart

Name _____

Valentine's Day

What comes between these pairs? Use your knowledge to fill in the missing links.
You may need to research a few.

1. Mars _____ Saturn

2. Utah _____ California

3. XXXIII _____ XXXV

4. computer keyboard C _____ B

5. Norway _____ Finland

6. touchtone phone #2 _____ #8

7. North America _____ South America

8. earth's crust _____ earth's core

9. dō (musical scale) _____ mi

10. 2nd baseman _____ 3rd baseman

11. Central time zone _____ Pacific time zone

12. July _____ September

13. insect head _____ insect abdomen

14. British Columbia _____ Saskatchewan

15. $1 George Washington _____ $10 Alexander Hamilton

16. Mt. Rushmore Jefferson _____ Lincoln

17. phlanges _____ tarsals (bones of foot)

18. Spanish number *uno* _____ tres

Pair 'Em Up

Name _____

Valentine's Day

February is the shortest month of the year, even during Leap Year. Abbreviations are shortened forms of longer words. Match the words in the left column to the abbreviations on the right. Place the correct letter in front of each number. Not every word in the second column will be used.

____ 1. street   a. oz.
____ 2. doctor   b. Ave.
____ 3. post office   c. lb.
____ 4. mister   d. St.
____ 5. road   e. Wed.
____ 6. ounce   f. Mr.
____ 7. junior   g. Mt.
____ 8. avenue   h. cm
____ 9. October   i. ft.
____ 10. foot   j. Dr.
____ 11. Wednesday   k. pps.
____ 12. pound   l. pd.
____ 13. mountain   m. Oct.
____ 14. centimeter   n. Rd.
                        o. Jr.
                        p. P.O.

MAYBE YOU COULD RAISE A HERD OF NAUGAS FOR LIKE, Y'KNOW... NAUGAHYDE!

IF8727 *Challenge Your Mind*

Cupid's Capers

Name _____

Create a crazy story! Fold this page on the dotted line. While the right side is out of sight, write words in the blanks on the left. Then unfold the page and place your words in the story. Read it to a friend.

1. _____
   your birthday

2. _____
   a feeling

3. _____
   adjective

4. _____
   noun

5. _____
   plural noun

6. _____
   classmate–boy

7. _____
   classmate–girl

8. _____
   future year

9. _____
   plural noun

10. _____
    verb

11. _____
    color

12. _____
    color

13. _____
    plural noun

14. _____
    adjective

Valentine's Day this year will be celebrated on

_____ . The holiday honors _____ . Cupid was
   1   2

the Roman god of _____ . He is often pictured as a
                      2

_____ _____ . Cupid carries a curved bow
   3   4

which shoots out _____ . If the _____ hit
                      5   5

_____ and _____ , they will have a crush on
   6   7

each other until _____ . If Cupid misses his aim,
                      8

_____ will fall from the heavens and _____
   9   10

upon all of the people.

    When you write your Valentine cards this year,

remember Cupid and his favorite verse.

Roses are _____ ,
              11

Violets are _____ ,
               12

Cupid shoots _____ ,
                13

His Valentines are _____ .
                      14

CUPID IS ALSO KNOWN
AS EROS OR AMOR!

Dream Maker

Name _____

Inside the boxes, write the words that fit each shape to complete this story about Martin Luther King, Jr., a famous black American. The Word Bank will help you.

Martin Luther King, Jr., was born in _____, Georgia, on _____ 15, 1929. He loved school and was so _____ that he skipped two grades and graduated when he was _____. He studied to become a _____ like his father. In 1954, he became pastor of a church in _____, _____. There he worked hard to gain rights for black Americans. In 1956, blacks and whites rode buses _____ in Montgomery, Alabama for the first time. Afterward, President John F. _____ asked congress to pass civil rights legislation. King gave his _____ "I-Have-a-Dream" _____ at the march on _____ on August 28, 1963. Although he was _____ and people threatened to harm him for his _____, he continued to preach nonviolence. He wanted a _____ world for all races. He was assassinated in _____, Tennessee, on April 4, 1968. His birthday was declared a national holiday in 1986.

Word Bank

Montgomery · Kennedy · January · Washington · intelligent · famous · minister · together · arrested · peaceful · Memphis · beliefs · Alabama · Atlanta · speech · fifteen

© Instructional Fair • TS Denison

IF8727 *Challenge Your Mind*

ABE-GORIES

name _____

Presidents' Day

Abraham Lincoln was the sixteenth president of the United States. On February 12, 1809, he was born in a log cabin in Kentucky, and he is honored on Presidents' Day. Honor Mr. Lincoln by completing this chart. Write words to fit each category using letters shown at the top of each column. Fill in as many words as you can in each box. You may use information sources to help your search. Then compare your answers to two or three classmates' answers, crossing out any words that are the same. Determine which person has the most items unmarked.

Category	L	O	G	S
Major U.S. cities				
U.S. States				
Countries of the World				

ABE LINCOLN'S FATHER WAS A SKILLED CARPENTER AND PURCHASED THREE FARMS IN KENTUCKY BEFORE THE LINCOLNS MOVED TO INDIANA!

By George

Name _____

Fill in the blanks using scrambled choices from the Word Box to learn more about the man who is known in American history as "Father of the Country."

Word Bank

a n i r i V g i	k a b s e o r h c	y a r o l v t u e i n o R
s e r o h s	c i t h m e r i t a	l p i t a c a
n d i l h c d a r n g r e	n i n t a l p t a o	g o t a b n i
n i t e f n i c o	g i h f s n i	l a r n e G e
r a m o j	s e u o H h W t e i	k s r w o r o n i

George Washington was born in the state of _____ . At the age of 3, his family moved to a large _____ called Mt. Vernon. Then when he was seven, the family moved to Ferry Farm close to his father's _____ . As a schoolboy, George's favorite subject was _____ . George had a lifelong love of _____ . He enjoyed hunting, _____ , and _____ on the river.

In 1752, George decided to join the military. He was commissioned a _____ and was asked to train other soldiers. Eventually he was given the title of _____ of the Armies of the United States.

George married a widow named Martha Custis at her Virginia plantation called the _____ _____ . Martha and George raised her two children and later raised two _____ whose father died during the _____ War.

After two terms as President, George helped plan the new U.S. _____ which was named in his honor.

Washington died at age 67 when he got a throat _____ after riding _____ in the snow.

1-800-Mush

Name _____

Iditarod Race

Fill in the blanks with words from the Word Bank.

Word Bank

transport	Nome	medicines	Anchorage
dog mushing	difficult	life-saving	finish line
Iditarod			diptheria

Every March, a sled dog race takes place in Alaska called the _____ . It originated when _____ was used to _____ vaccines over 1,000 miles of rough terrain. These _____ were needed to fight a disease called _____ , so their mission was truly a _____ one. Today's race is in memory of that run. This _____ race is 1,049 miles long. The trip begins in _____ , and the dogs cross the _____ on Front Street in _____ , Alaska.

THE HUSKY IS THE SLED DOG OF CHOICE! MUSH!

IF8727 *Challenge Your Mind*

Ask the Doctor

name _____

Dr. Seuss's Birthday

Born on March 2, 1904 in Springfield, Massachusetts, Dr. Seuss wrote over 50 books for children. Match the clues with the correct titles to fill in the boxes. Then read the highlighted boxes vertically to learn Dr. Seuss' birth name.

Titles List

Fox In Socks
Butter Battle Book
Horton Hears a Who
Yertle the Turtle
How the Grinch Stole Christmas
The Cat in the Hat
Boom Boom Boom

Daisy Head Mayzie
Thidwick the Big-Hearted Moose
Green Eggs & Ham
Horton Hatches the Egg
Bartholomew & the Oobleck
The King's Stilts
King's Beard

1. Male produces oval-shaped object
2. feline with headgear
3. shelled animal with rhyming name
4. male with green goop
5. female with floral head
6. loud noises
7. male with auditory gift
8. royalty's whiskers
9. quadruped with large, beating organ
10. grass-colored breakfast food
11. tall walking sticks belonging to royalty
12. carnivorous animal with foot warmers
13. ogre steals December holiday
14. fight of the bread spread

© Instructional Fair • TS Denison   23   IF8727 Challenge Your Mind

The Birthday Bell

name _____

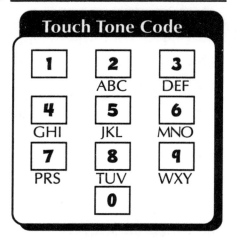

Alexander Graham Bell's Birthday.

Call waiting! Redial! Alexander Graham Bell would be surprised at the changes to the telephone since his invention was patented in March 1876. Use the Touch Tone Code to discover some fun phone facts.
(**Example:** 2 = C, 2 = A, 2 = B)

Touch Tone Code

1	2 ABC	3 DEF
4 GHI	5 JKL	6 MNO
7 PRS	8 TUV	9 WXY
	0	

1. Alexander's home country was 7 2 6 8 5 2 6 3 . _____

2. After coming to the United States in 1871, he taught people who were deaf

   in 2 6 7 8 6 6. _____

3. The invention of the telephone happened quite by 2 2 2 4 3 3 6 8 .

   _____

4. Bell spilled 2 2 8 8 3 7 9   2 2 4 3   _____

   _____ on his clothes.

5. He then called, " 6 7.   9 2 8 7 6 6,   2 6 6 3   4 3 7 3 .

   _____ _____ , _____ _____ I want you."

6. Watson heard the first actual 8 7 2 6 7 6 4 8 8 3 3 _____
   speech.

7. The first telephone company, 2 3 5 5   8 3 5 3 7 4 6 6 3

   2 6 6 7 2 6 9 _____ _____ _____

   began in July, 1877.

8. Bell filed his patent just a few hours before   3 5 4 7 4 2   4 7 2 9

   _____ _____ , another American inventor, whom

   Western Union claimed had invented the telephone first.

Mardi Gras Madness

Name _____

Mardi Gras

Create a crazy story! Fold this page on the dotted line. While the right side is out of sight, write words in the blanks on the left. Then unfold the page and place your word choices in the story. Share your creation with a friend.

1. _____
   your teacher
2. _____
   type of transportation
3. _____
   length of time
4. _____
   noun
5. _____
   classmate
6. _____
   adjective
7. _____
   number
8. _____
   adjective
9. _____
   plural noun
10. _____
    plural noun
11. _____
    adjective
12. _____
    plural noun
13. _____
    boy classmate
14. _____
    verb (past)

Our teacher, _____ , took us on a magical Mardi Gras field trip. We traveled by _____ . It took us _____ to get to New Orleans. When we unpacked, I discovered that I had forgotten my _____ , so I had to borrow one from _____ . We stayed in a _____ hotel with _____ floors. Each room had a little balcony overlooking _____ streets where groups of _____ roamed all day and night.

   The highlight of our trip was the day of the Mardi Gras parade. People in the parade wore masks made of _____ . Their clothes were very _____ . As the floats passed, the passengers threw us necklaces made of _____ . _____ really looked weird in a necklace! When all of the excitement was over, we walked back to our hotel, where we _____ until 3:00 in the morning! It was a trip we will never forget!

SAY WHAT.....?!

Happy Birthday Albert!

Name _____

Albert Einstein's Birthday

Albert Einstein is best remembered as a leading scientific thinker in the field of physics. The anniversary of his birthday is March 14. Today the field of science offers many career opportunities. Use the code box to match the job descriptions with the career titles.

CODE BOX	A	B	C	D	E	F	G	H	I	J	K	L	M
	3	26	11	7	4	23	12	14	2	22	16	8	18
	N	O	P	Q	R	S	T	U	V	W	X	Y	Z
	9	1	15	20	5	19	6	10	25	13	24	17	21

1. I study animal life.

   _____
   (21 – 1 – 1 – 8 – 1 – 12 – 2 – 19 – 6)

2. Using our natural resources properly is my main concern.

   _____
   (11 – 1 – 9 – 19 – 4 – 5 – 25 – 3 – 6 – 2 – 1 – 9 – 2 – 19 – 6)

3. I design circuitry.

   _____
   (4 – 8 – 4 – 11 – 6 – 5 – 2 – 11 – 2 – 3 – 9)

4. I study plant life.

   _____
   (26 – 1 – 6 – 3 – 9 – 2 – 19 – 6)

5. The universe is my area of study.

   _____
   (3 – 19 – 6 – 5 – 1 – 9 – 1 – 18 – 4 – 5)

6. I study the origin of human beings. _____
   (3 – 9 – 6 – 14 – 5 – 1 – 15 – 1 – 8 – 1 – 12 – 2 – 19 – 6)

7. I mix different kinds of matter to make new materials.

   _____
   (11 – 14 – 4 – 18 – 2 – 19 – 6)

8. I study and forecast weather.

   _____
   (18 – 4 – 6 – 4 – 1 – 5 – 1 – 8 – 1 – 12 – 2 – 19 – 6)

9. Rocks and minerals are my interests.

   _____
   (12 – 4 – 1 – 8 – 1 – 12 – 2 – 19 – 6)

10. I design machines using heat and power.

    _____
    (18 – 4 – 11 – 14 – 3 – 9 – 2 – 11 – 3 – 8

    _____
    4 – 9 – 12 – 2 – 9 – 4 – 4 – 5)

IF8727 *Challenge Your Mind*

McKerry O'Grid, the Leprechaun Kid

Name _____

St. Patrick's Day

Sure 'N Begorra, no St. Patrick's Day would be complete without knowing the language of the leprechauns. Use the grid to decode these Irish words, places, and phrases. The first coordinate given is the horizontal row of numbers. The first word has been done for you.

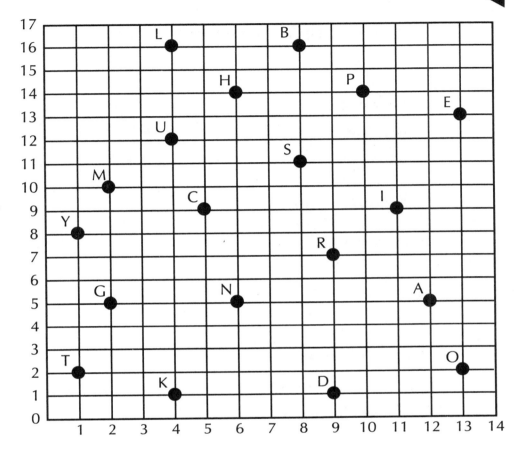

1. $\underset{8,16}{B}$ $\underset{4,16}{L}$ $\underset{12,5}{A}$ $\underset{9,7}{R}$ $\underset{6,5}{N}$ $\underset{13,13}{E}$ $\underset{1,8}{Y}$ $\underset{8,11}{S}$ $\underset{1,2}{T}$ $\underset{13,2}{O}$ $\underset{6,5}{N}$ $\underset{13,13}{E}$

2. ___ ___ ___ ___ ___ ___ ___ ___
   8,11 6,14 12,5 2,10 9,7 13,2 5,9 4,1

3. ___ ___ ___ ___ ___ ___ ___ ___ ___ ___
   8,11 6,14 11,9 4,16 4,16 13,13 4,16 12,5 2,5 6,14

4. ___ ___ ___ ___ ___ ___ ___   ___ ___ ___ ___
   13,13 2,10 13,13 9,7 12,5 4,16 9,1   11,9 8,11 4,16 13,13

5. ___ ___ ___ ___ ___ ___ ___ ___ ___
   4,1 11,9 4,16 4,16 12,5 9,7 6,5 13,13 1,8

6. ___ ___ ___ ___ ___ ___ ___ ___ ___ ___
   4,16 13,13 10,14 9,7 13,13 5,9 6,14 12,5 4,12 6,5

7. ___ ___ ___ ___ ___ ___ ___
   8,16 13,13 2,5 13,2 9,7 9,7 12,5

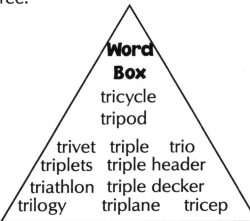

March "Tri"umphs

name _____

St. Patrick's Day

St. Patrick's Day honors the patron saint of Ireland who died on March 17. Many people believe St. Patrick used the shamrock to illustrate the idea of the trinity to Christians. Use the Word Box to help you complete the words beginning with "tri," which means three.

Word Box

tricycle
tripod
trivet   triple   trio
triplets   triple header
triathlon   triple decker
trilogy   triplane   tricep

1. athletic contest with swimming, bicycling, and running events   __ __ __ __ __ __ __ __ __

2. singing group of 3 people   __ __ __ __

3. three-legged camera stand   __ __ __ __ __ __

4. three-base hit in baseball   __ __ __ __ __ __

5. three-layered sandwich   __ __ __ __ __ __   __ __ __ __ __ __

6. three games or events in a row   __ __ __ __ __ __   __ __ __ __ __ __

7. three babies born at the same time   __ __ __ __ __ __ __ __

8. three-legged stand for a hot dish   __ __ __ __ __ __

9. three-headed muscle of the upper arm   __ __ __ __ __ __

10. series of three books on same theme by the same author   __ __ __ __ __ __ __

11. three-wheeled bicycle   __ __ __ __ __ __ __ __

12. airplane with wings above each other in 3 levels   __ __ __ __ __ __ __ __

IF8727 *Challenge Your Mind*

Wearin' o' the Green

Name _____

St. Patrick's Day

What is your "Green IQ" for March? Use the definitions below to help you identify each one. Have your teacher read the answers. For each correct answer score the number of points shown. Total the points to determine your Green IQ.

1. U.S. paper money nickname   **G R E E n** __ __ __ __ (3)

2. a fir or pine tree   __ __ __ __ **G R E E n** (1)

3. a minty flavor   __ __ __ __ __ __ **G R E E n** (2)

4. a glass-sided building for plant growing   **G R E E n** __ __ __ __ (1)

5. ID card for a foreigner with permanent residence in the U.S.   **G R E E n** __ __ __ __ (3)

6. the Prime Meridian passes through it   **G R E E n** __ __ __ __ (2)

7. an inexperienced person   **G R E E n** __ __ __ __ (2)

8. Is the moon really made of this?   **G R E E n** __ __ __ __ __ __ (1)

9. world's largest island—near Canada   **G R E E n** __ __ __ __ (1)

10. gardening "know how"   **G R E E n** __ __ __ __ (2)

11. a traffic signal meaning "Go"   **G R E E n** __ __ __ __ (1)

12. plants or foliage   **G R E E n** __ __ __ (2)

13. jealousy   **G R E E n** - __ __ __ __ (2)

14. special U.S. military forces   **G R E E n** __ __ __ __ __ __ (3)

wintergreen	green card	evergreen	greenery
Greenwich	greenhorn	Greenland	greenback
green cheese	green light	greenhouse	green-eyed
green thumb	Green Berets		

Total Score: _____
A perfect "Green IQ" score totals 26 points.

© Instructional Fair • TS Denison

29

IF8727 Challenge Your Mind

Medieval March

Name _____

Become acquainted with the Middle Ages in March. Research the knightly terms to work the puzzle.

Across

1. customs of medieval knighthood
2. King Arthur's sword
3. King Arthur's circular table
4. a knightly martial sport
5. combat on horseback
6. magician of King Arthur's court
7. steel-tipped spear of a knight
8. water-filled trench around a castle
9. a feudal tenant

Down

1. armor bearer for a knight
2. a young boy who desires to become a knight
3. the church seat of the bishop
4. a successful squire becomes one
5. metallic body covering
6. an establishment for monks
7. a medieval brother
8. a symbolic emblem (3 words)
9. a large, fortified building

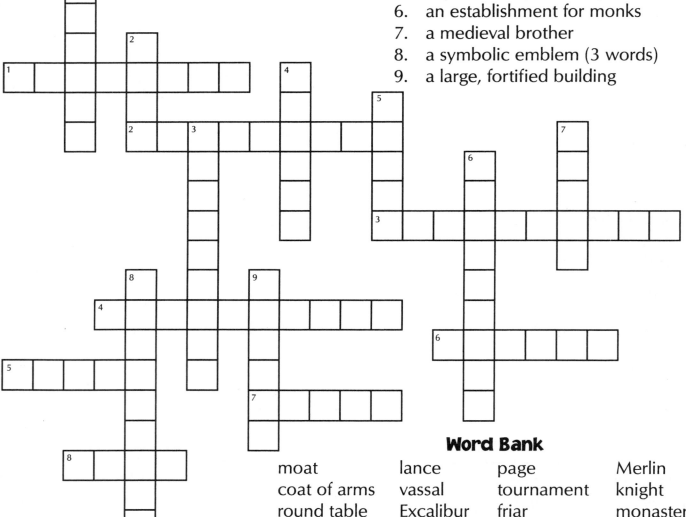

Word Bank

moat	lance	page	Merlin
coat of arms	vassal	tournament	knight
round table	Excalibur	friar	monastery
squire	armor	joust	castle
chivalry	cathedral		

Don't Be Fooled

Name _____

April Fools' Day

COULD YOU, LIKE, YOU KNOW... REPEAT THE QUESTION?

Let's see how much you know. Answer each question very carefully.

1. Who sits in the chair at the Lincoln Memorial? _____

2. Where was the Korean War fought? _____

3. How many days are in a seven-day week? _____

4. In what city do the Chicago Bulls play? _____

5. What is the product of 9 x 8 x 7 x 6 x 5 x 4 x 3 x 2 x 1 x 0? _____

6. If a plane crashed exactly on the border between the U.S. and Canada, where would the survivors be buried? _____

7. Which state is the Mississippi River named after? _____

8. Which weighs more, a pound of dust or a pound of rocks? _____

9. How do you spell *intelligence*? _____

10. Who wrote the autobiography of Benjamin Franklin? _____

11. Who is buried in Grant's tomb? _____

12. What are JFK's initials? _____

13. How many months have 28 days? _____

14. How long is a four-minute TV commercial? _____

15. How many pennies are in an empty piggy bank? _____

16. How many pickled peppers did Peter Piper pick? _____

17. What fills a helium balloon? _____

18. What color is the White House in Washington, D.C.? _____

IF8727 *Challenge Your Mind*

Fools' Day Fun

name _____

An eleven-word phase is hidden in the puzzle below. Unscramble the letters by moving one letter in any direction. You may use each letter only once.

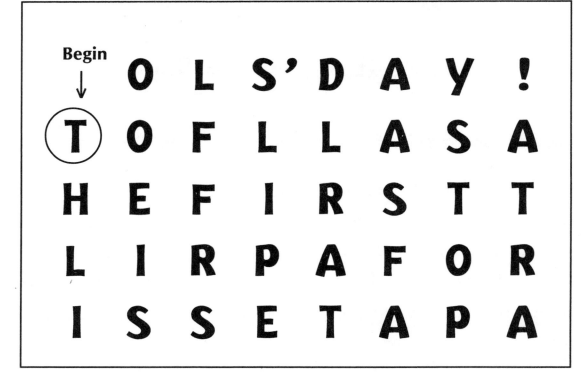

Begin

O L S' D A Y !
T O F L L A S A
H E F I R S T T
L I R P A F O R
I S S E T A P A

Answer:

_____

_____

THE FEAST OF FOOLS WAS A MOCK RELIGIOUS FESTIVAL HELD IN ENGLAND AND FRANCE FROM THE 5TH TO THE 16TH CENTURIES!

IF8727 *Challenge Your Mind*

Bogus Bloomers

name _____

April Fools' Day

April gets its name from the Latin word *Aprilis* meaning to open. Flowers often open or bloom in April. Meet the "famous" gardeners who tend these flowers. Unscramble their names to form the real names of flowers. The first one is done for you. Fold back the top of the page and see how many you can solve without the help of the Word Box.

Word Box

aster	poppy	hyacinth	carnation
zinnia	bluebell	petunia	daisies
violet	orchid	daffodil	poinsettia
tulips	sunflower	marigold	

1. Walt Reily   *water lily*
2. Lu Spit   _____
3. Fil Fodda   _____
4. Sue Flowrn   _____
5. Vi Tole   _____
6. Cinty Hah   _____
7. Bub Lelel   _____
8. Sid Easi   _____

9. Doc Hir   _____
10. Stepia Toni   _____
11. Anna Trico   _____
12. Izi Ann   _____
13. Ina Tupe   _____
14. Marg Oldi   _____
15. P. P. Poy   _____
16. St. Ear   _____

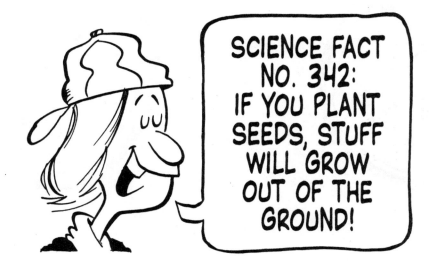

SCIENCE FACT NO. 342: IF YOU PLANT SEEDS, STUFF WILL GROW OUT OF THE GROUND!

© Instructional Fair • TS Denison

-33-

IF8727 *Challenge Your Mind*

Are You Stumped?

Name _____

Arbor Day

On Arbor Day, schoolchildren are encouraged to plant trees. This day was first established by Julius Sterling Morton, a Nebraska newspaper publisher, who discovered that trees would enrich and conserve moisture in the soil. A tree-related word is scrambled in each section of the tree stump. Find the letter that is missing from each word. Write that letter in the center. Write the four words below each stump.

Kinds of trees

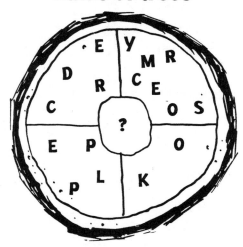

_____   _____

_____   _____

Fruit from trees

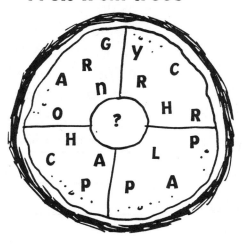

_____   _____

_____   _____

Tree parts

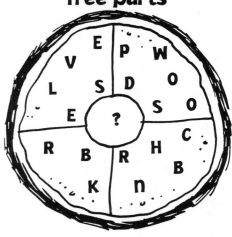

_____   _____

_____   _____

Necessities for growth

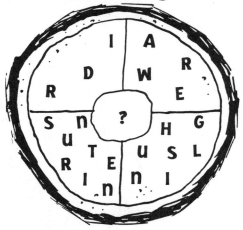

_____   _____

_____   _____

Seeing Double

Name _____

April—Spring

Bunny rabbits! Spring offers an array of double letters. Use the clues to write a word with double letters.

1. dustlike sparkles

2. light rain
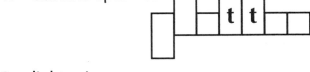

3. soft, airy

4. textbook dictionary
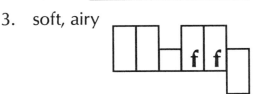

5. to help

6. leaping
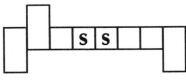

7. brown, sticky syrup
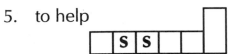

8. every year
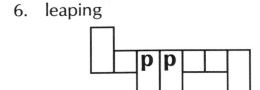

9. red and white striped candy
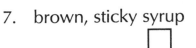

10. tells when guests arrive
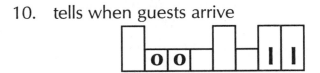

11. pigskin sport
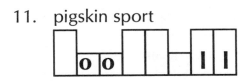

12. rapid repetitive talking
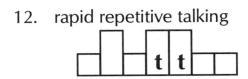

13. to eat quickly
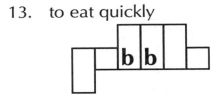

14. book pictures

15. where you live
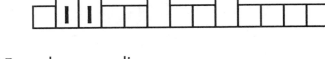

16. lines that never cross
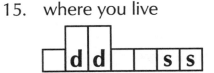
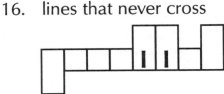

IF8727 *Challenge Your Mind*

Presto!

name _____

Easter

Abracadabra . . .   Oops! When the magician pulled these alphabet strips from his top hat, some of the letters were missing. First write the missing alphabet letters. Then unscramble them to form a word. Do this for each alphabet strip. Fill in the blanks with words from above to answer the riddle.

1.
R	C	Q	G	S	U	I	B	L	V
H	F	K	A	J	X	P	O	D	M

___ ___ ___ ___ ___ ___   ___ ___ ___ ___ I ___

(missing letters)   (word)

2.
Q	H	M	Z	C	I	R	D	X	T	L	S
B	U	F	J	P	Y	G	V	W	K	A	

___ ___ ___ ___   ___ ___ ___ ___

(missing letters)   (word)

3.
E	J	O	Q	G	V	Z	I	T	C	A
K	R	H	D	P	S	M	X	L	F	W

___ ___ ___ ___ ___   ___ ___ n ___

(missing letters)   (word)

4.
B	K	O	X	I	D	Q	V	Y	G
H	P	M	C	R	W	Z	J	F	N

___ ___ ___ ___ ___ ___ ___ ___   ___ ___ ___ ___ ___ ___

(missing letters)   (word)

> **How do rabbits honor those who have gone to the "hare"-after?**

With a . . .

1. ___ ___ ___ ___ I ___   -   2. ___ ___ ___ ___   3. " ___ ___ ___ n ___ "

4. ___ ___ ___ ___ ___ ___

IF8727 *Challenge Your Mind*

Keep Your Bunny Side Up!

Name _____ Easter

Use the Word Box to help you solve these teasers.

1. rabbit wedding march _____

2. how rabbits order their eggs _____

3. where newly married rabbits go _____

4. what bunny nuns wear _____

5. why Grandma Bunny wore a wig _____

6. expensive bunny jewelry _____

7. bunny light green cantaloupe _____

8. what deaf bunnies wear _____

9. a narrow escape for rabbits _____

10. carrots passed down from generation to generation _____

11. rabbit heaven _____

12. what bunny cooks must wear _____

13. rabbit jet travel _____

14. James Howe vampire rabbit _____

15. bunny fur groomer _____

16. a comical hare _____

Word Box

haring aid	bunny dew melon	14-carrot gold
hare net	hare-raising experience	hare-itage
"Hare Comes the Bride"	bunny side up	funny bunny
too many gray hares	the hare after	Bunnicula
hare dryer	rabbit habit	hare plane
on a bunny moon		

Earth First

name _____

Earth Day

Find the path with a message about the earth. Highlight the message from one side of the puzzle to another.

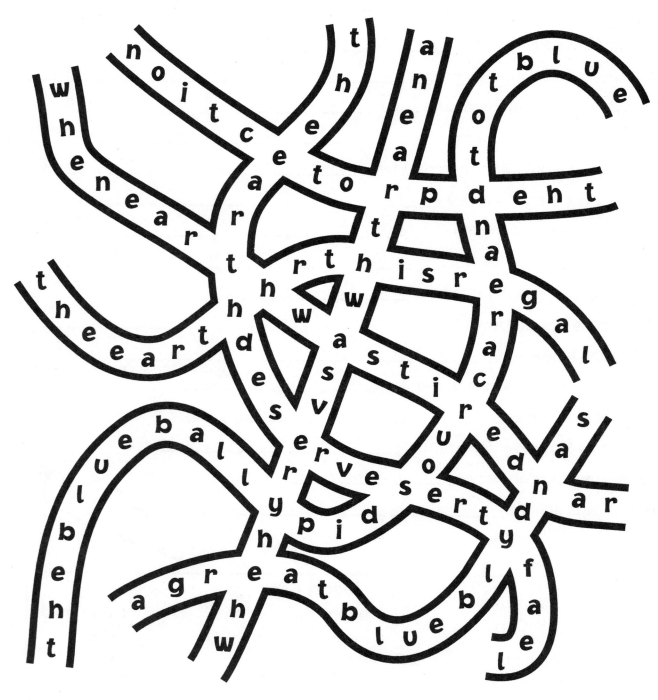

Message:

_____

April Firsts

name _____

Samuel Morse's Birthday

Samuel Morse was born on April 27, 1791 and is best known for developing the first successful electric telegraph. Decode the messages about April events using the Morse Code.

Morse Code

A ●—	E ●	I ●●	M ——	Q ——●—	U ●●—	Y —●——
B —●●●	F ●●—●	J ●———	N —●	R ●—●	V ●●●—	Z ——●●
C —●—●	G ——●	K —●—	O ———	S ●●●	W ●——	
D —●●	H ●●●●	L ●—●●	P ●——●	T —	X —●●—	

April 2   Juan Ponce de Leon discovered ●●—●/●—●●/———/●—●/●●/—●●/●— in 1513. _____

April 3   In 1860, the ●——●/———/—●/—●—— ●/—●●—/●——●/●—●/●/●●●/●●● began. _____

April 6   In 1896, the first ———/●—●●/—●——/——/●——●/●●/—●—● ——●/●—/———/●/●●● were held in Athens, Greece.

_____

April 8   In 1974, ●●●●/●—/—●/—●— ●—/●—/●—●/———/—● broke Babe Ruth's record of 714 home runs. _____

April 14   In 1865, ●—/—●●●/● ●—●●/●●/—●/—●—●/———/●—●●/—● was assassinated. _____

April 18   In 1775, ●——●/●—/●●—/●—●● ●—●/●/●●●—/●/●—●/● made his famous ride. _____

April 24   In 1704, the first American —●/●/●——/●●●/●——●/●—/●——●/●/●—● was regularly published. _____

IF8727 *Challenge Your Mind*

A-May-zing Month

Name _____

April showers brought these May flowers. Use the Word Box to help you write words that have "May" as part of the answer.

Word Box

dismay   Mayas
mayday   mayhem
Mayflower   mayonnaise
mayapple   maybe
maypole   mayor

1. an Indian group of the Yucatan, Honduras, Guatemala, El Salvador, and Belize
   MAY __ __

2. American herb of barberry family
   MAY __ __ __ __ __

3. international radio telephone distress signal
   MAY __ __ __

4. possibly
   MAY __ __

5. willful damage or violence
   MAY __ __ __

6. salad dressing
   MAY __ __ __ __ __ __ __

7. elected city head
   MAY __ __

8. flowered pole for dancing around
   MAY __ __ __ __

9. sudden loss of courage
   __ __ __ MAY

10. the Pilgrims' ship
    MAY __ __ __ __ __

I Have My Pride, After All

Name _____

Be Kind to Animals Week

The first week in May is "Be Kind to Animals Week." Groups of animals are described with many different words. Use the code in the box below to identify each group of animals. Write the word on the blank.

HOW ABOUT A GIGGLE OF GIRLS?!

Code Box

A	B	C	D	E	F	G	H	I	J	K	L	M
2	15	10	7	3	17	11	21	1	23	18	8	13

N	O	P	Q	R	S	T	U	V	W	X	Y	Z
24	4	14	22	12	6	9	5	16	25	19	20	26

1. a (17 – 8 – 4 – 10 – 18) of chickens _____

2. a (18 – 3 – 24 – 24 – 3 – 8) of dogs _____

3. a (6 – 10 – 21 – 4 – 4 –8) of fish _____

4. a (6 – 18 – 5 – 8 – 18) of foxes _____

5. a (11 – 2 – 11 – 11 – 8 – 3) of geese _____

6. a (10 – 4 – 8 – 4 – 24 – 20) of ants _____

7. a (14 – 4 – 7) of whales _____

8. a (14 – 2 – 10 – 3) of donkeys _____

9. a (14 – 12 – 1 – 7 – 3) of lions _____

10. a (25 – 2 – 12 – 12 – 3 – 24) of rabbits _____

11. a (21 – 3 – 12 – 7) of cattle _____

12. a (10 – 8 – 4 – 25 – 7 – 3 – 12) of cats _____

13. a (13 – 4 – 15) of kangaroos _____

14. a (14 – 2 – 10 – 18) of wolves _____

IF8727 *Challenge Your Mind*

"Cat-chy" Animal Expressions

Name _____

Be Kind to Animals Week

Match these animal expressions with their meanings by writing the letters on the blanks.

_____ 1. crocodile tears
_____ 2. duck
_____ 3. guinea pig
_____ 4. bee
_____ 5. eager beaver
_____ 6. to rat on
_____ 7. hold your horses
_____ 8. play possum
_____ 9. clam up
_____ 10. get your goat
_____ 11. horse around
_____ 12. sheepish
_____ 13. the cat's meow
_____ 14. fishy
_____ 15. a bear
_____ 16. turkey
_____ 17. quick as a rabbit

a. pretend to be asleep or dead
b. a spelling contest
c. play
d. to tell on someone
e. bothers you
f. to go underwater
g. suspicious
h. foolish person
i. someone anxious to do something
j. shy, embarrassed
k. fake crying
l. terrific
m. wait patiently
n. be quiet
o. something really difficult
p. someone who tries something first
q. fast

THE FIRST AMERICAN SOCIETY FOR THE PREVENTION OF CRUELTY TO ANIMALS WAS CHARTERED IN NEW YORK IN 1866!

May Daze

Name _____

May

Try to figure out the word or phrase represented by these puzzles. Write answers under each box. The first one is done for you.

1.
Strike
   Strike
      Strike
y o u' r e

__three strikes,__
__you're out__

2.
m ce
m ce
m ce

_____

3.

_____

4.
b   b
u   q
t h t

_____

5.
weather
   cast
   cast
   cast
   cast

_____

6.
tire

_____

7.
FIVE

_____

8.
SHOE
SHOE

_____

9.
E
L
K
C
U
B

_____

10.
LIPS

Lips

_____

11.
$ NUTS

_____

12.
¢ ipede

_____

13.
2th DK

_____

14.
WI   NG

_____

15.
D K I

_____

16.
S P A C E

_____

IF8727 *Challenge Your Mind*

Who Said It?

1st Comic Strip
Appeared in
Newspapers—
May 6, 1847

To identify famous cartoon characters, write the letter of the alphabet that comes after each letter (after **Z** return to **A**). Then cut out a speech bubble and match it with the cartoon character who might have made that comment.

GNAADR _____	FZQEHDKC _____	CDMMHR the LDMZBD _____
RMNNOX _____	ATFR ATMMX _____	YHFFX _____
RTODQLZM _____	SVDDSX AHQC _____	LHBJDX LNTRD _____

Meet my buddy, Woodstock.

Watch me get Odie!

I tawt I taw a puddy tat!

I'll change in this phone booth.

Where are you, Calvin?

Mr. Wilson, where are you?

I'm "all ears," Minnie.

What's up, Doc?

Nothing ever goes right for me.

44

Diamond Dust

Name _____

Baseball Season

Create a crazy story! Fold this page on the dotted line. While the right side is out of sight, write words in the blanks on the left. Then unfold the page and place your word choices on the appropriate lines in the story! Share your creation with a friend.

1. _____
   city

2. _____
   plural noun

3. _____
   classmate

4. _____
   noun

5. _____
   number

6. _____
   two classmates

7. _____
   verb (present tense)

8. _____
   number

9. _____
   body part (plural)

10. _____
    city

11. _____
    expression

12. _____
    adjective

13. _____
    dollar amount

14. _____
    food item

Baseball season is back! This year there's a hot new team called the _____ _____ . Their ace pitcher, _____ , has a _____ for an arm. His/her fastball speeds in at _____ miles per hour. In the dugout are two more walking wizards, _____ and _____ . One of them, however, has bad wheels and can only _____ around the base paths. The other throws smoke, often fanning _____ batters in a single inning!

1   2
3   4
5
6
6
7
8

That ball not only has eyes, it has _____ !
And who keeps the batter's box neat? Why, the cleanup hitter, of course. Speaking of hitters, this team's sluggers can hit them clean to _____ . When they do, a roar goes up from the crowd, yelling _____ . So far their season is off to a _____ start, so come on out to see them. Tickets only cost _____ , and there's plenty of _____ to eat.

9
10
11
12
13   14

Lastly, do you know why the rookie had coal on his face? He came from the "miners"!

Play ball!

IF8727 *Challenge Your Mind*

Lest We Forget

Memorial Day

Memorial Day is a patriotic holiday celebrated on the last Monday in May to honor our country's citizens who died defending the U.S.A. Number each group of words in alphabetical order. Write the first letter of the number-two word in the matching blank below. The first two are done for you.

1. ★ **2** enemy
   1 eagle
   3 forge

2. ★ **2** Marines
   3 party
   1 main

3. ___ united
   ___ weak
   ___ weapons

4. ___ honor
   ___ infantry
   ___ honest

5. ___ defend
   ___ grave
   ___ dedication

6. ___ parade
   ___ Marine
   ___ parody

7. ___ glory
   ___ headstone
   ___ heard

8. ___ annual
   ___ amnesty
   ___ American

9. ___ monuments
   ___ memorial
   ___ open

10. ___ Uncle
    ___ treaty
    ___ Sam

11. ___ valor
    ___ tactics
    ___ veterans

12. ___ yearn
    ___ Yankee
    ___ violent

13. ___ yesterday
    ___ peace
    ___ youth

14. ___ religion
    ___ respect
    ___ soldier

15. ___ stars
    ___ yesteryear
    ___ youth

16. ___ salute
    ___ taps
    ___ tribute

17. ___ gravestone
    ___ nation
    ___ loyalty

18. ___ armed forces
    ___ attack
    ___ freedom

19. ___ battle
    ___ enthusiasm
    ___ glory

20. ___ bugle
    ___ Arlington Cemetery
    ___ air raid

21. ___ tactics
    ___ honor
    ___ induction

22. ___ army
    ___ anger
    ___ bold

23. ___ forgive
    ___ educate
    ___ bravery

24. ___ epitaph
    ___ ceremony
    ___ flag

25. ___ dedicate
    ___ decorations
    ___ flowers

26. ___ peace
    ___ create
    ___ offer

___ ___ ___ ___   ___ ___ ___ **E** ___   ___ ___ ___   ___ ___ ___
10 4 24 15   6 20 11 1 25   16 7 23   3 18 12

For ___ ___ **M** ___ ___ ___ ___ ___   ___ ___ ___
        9 19 2 26 14 21 8 17   5 22 13

Palindrome Pals

Name _____

During May, we honor Mom on Mother's Day. Father's Day in June praises Pop.
The words mom and pop are called palindromes. These words are spelled the same
forward and backward. Use the clues to discover more palindromes.

1. a young dog   — — —
2. 12:00 P.M.   — — — —
3. horizontally even   — — — — — —
4. baby chick's sound   — — — —
5. to hang wall covering again   — — — — — — — —
6. horn sound   — — — —
7. a dipping into water for apples game   — — — —
8. the night before Christmas   — — —
9. pieces played alone   — — — — —
10. a musical engagement   — — — —
11. another name for pop   — — —
12. radio device to locate objects   — — — — —
13. Indy 500 vehicle (2 words)   — — — — — — —
14. a good work done by a scout   — — — —
15. a female sheep   — — —
16. tiny child   — — —
17. a joke played on someone   — — —
18. opposite of brother   — — — —
19. Great! Super!   — — — —
20. home of your iris and cornea   — — —

HOW
ABOUT
TOOT?

Challenge:

Cool palindrome sentences . . .

> Step on no pets!

Can you create more?

Too hot to hoot!

IF8727 *Challenge Your Mind*

Travel Time

name _____

Summer Vacation

Summer vacation is almost here. It's time to plan a trip or two. Think about packing, means of transportation, and destinations as you complete this chart. Write words to fit each category using letters shown at the top of each column. Fill in as many words as you can in each box. You may use information sources to help your search. Then compare your answers to two or three classmates' answers, crossing out any words that are the same. Determine which person has the most items un-marked.

Category	T	R	I	P	S
Destinations					
Items to pack					
Means of travel					

LET'S GO!!

IF8727 *Challenge Your Mind*

Crack the Cheese Code

Name _____

Count the holes in the pieces of cheese. Write that number beside the cheese. Then use the numbers to break the code. For example, if the number is $\overline{4}$, write the letter M. If the number is $\underline{4}$ write the letter J.

$\overline{4}$ $\underline{5}$ $\overline{5}$ $\underline{10}$ $\overline{0}$ $\overline{1}$ $\overline{2}$ $\overline{8}$ $\underline{10}$ $\overline{2}$ $\overline{0}$ $\overline{4}$ $\underline{10}$

$\overline{2}$ $\overline{8}$ $\overline{1}$ $\overline{7}$ $\underline{2}$ $\underline{5}$ $\overline{2}$ $\underline{10}$ $\overline{7}$ $\overline{4}$ $\underline{10}$ $\overline{3}$ $\underline{0}$ $\underline{1}$ $\overline{7}$ $\overline{5}$

$\overline{9}$ $\overline{7}$ $\underline{0}$ $\overline{3}$ $\overline{6}$ $\underline{9}$ $\overline{3}$ $\overline{8}$ $\overline{9}$ $\underline{5}$ $\underline{1}$ $\underline{10}$ $\overline{3}$ $\overline{1}$!

$\overline{9}$ $\underline{0}$ $\overline{9}$ $\overline{6}$ $\overline{8}$ $\underline{5}$ $\overline{3}$ $\overline{5}$ $\overline{8}$ $\overline{0}$ $\overline{2}$ $\underline{8}$ $\overline{7}$ $\overline{2}$ $\overline{7}$

$\overline{6}$ $\overline{8}$ $\overline{8}$ $\overline{9}$ $\overline{9}$ $\overline{7}$ $\underline{0}$ $\overline{3}$ $\overline{6}$ $\overline{1}$ $\overline{8}$ $\overline{0}$ $\overline{4}$ $\overline{7}$ $\overline{6}$

$\overline{0}$ $\underline{10}$ $\overline{0}$ $\underline{6}$ $\overline{8}$ $\underline{5}$ $\overline{9}$ $\overline{2}$ $\overline{8}$ 1,700 $\underline{9}$ $\overline{8}$ $\underline{5}$ $\overline{5}$ $\overline{9}$ $\overline{1}$

$\overline{7}$ $\overline{5}$ $\overline{9}$ $\underline{9}$ $\overline{3}$ $\overline{8}$ $\overline{9}$ $\underline{5}$ $\underline{1}$ $\underline{10}$ 2,300 $\underline{6}$ $\overline{7}$ $\overline{2}$ $\overline{2}$ $\overline{8}$ $\overline{5}$ $\overline{1}$

$\overline{8}$ $\overline{3}$ $\overline{4}$ $\overline{8}$ $\overline{3}$ $\underline{10}$ $\overline{8}$ $\underline{10}$ $\overline{4}$ $\underline{0}$ $\overline{2}$ $\overline{3}$ $\underline{0}$ $\overline{5}$

$\overline{7}$ $\overline{6}$ $\underline{10}$ $\overline{7}$ $\overline{3}$?

  IF8727 *Challenge Your Mind*

Annual Tradition

Name _____

On June 1 and 2, Chicago holds Donut Days. This annual tradition recalls the donuts served to doughboys by the Salvation Army during WWI. Use the letters around the doughnuts to discover the names of other objects that have holes. Write the name of the object under each doughnut.

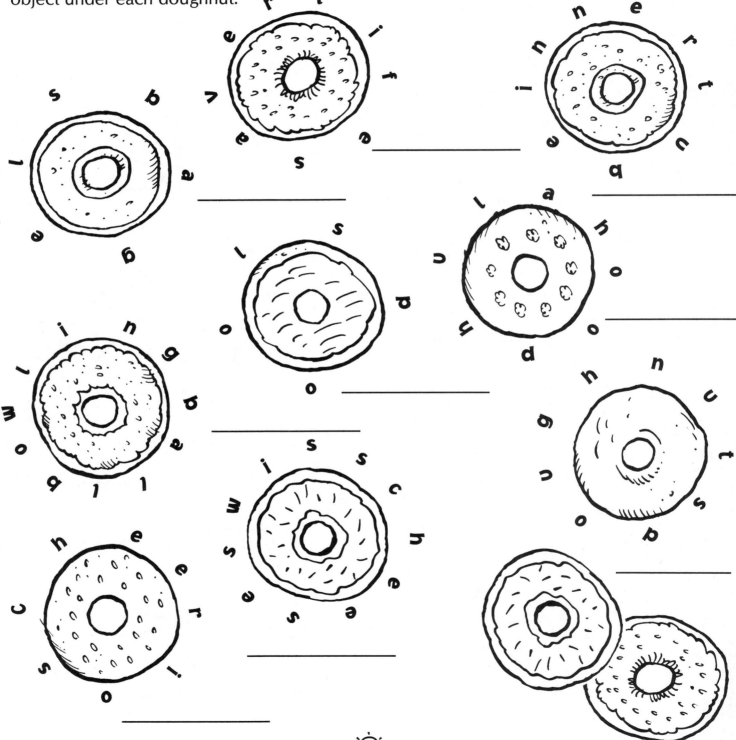

© Instructional Fair • TS Denison

IF8727 *Challenge Your Mind*

Patchwork Pals

Name _____

End of School Year

Celebrate the year's end with a pal search. Ask classmates to autograph boxes that apply to them. A student may not sign more than two times. The event had to happen during this school year.

_____ had a clean desk all year!	_____ outgrew some clothes.	_____ went on a field trip.	_____ had a parent visit the class.
_____ can name the 7 continents and 4 oceans.	_____ ate somewhere new.	_____ was in a play or recital.	_____ played soccer.
_____ wore red to school today.	_____ went to a basketball game.	_____ went on a weekend trip.	_____ went to a concert.
_____ helped the teacher.	_____ new to our school this year.	_____ made the class laugh.	_____ went home from school sick.
_____ got new shoes.	_____ got braces on teeth.	_____ got a haircut.	_____ can correctly spell a word with 10 letters or more.
_____ played on a school sports team.	_____ got a new pet.	_____ never missed a day of school.	_____ moved to a new house or apartment.

Happy Birthday U.S.

name _____

Each year on the fourth of July, the United States celebrates its birthday and the adoption of the Declaration of Independence. Solve these rebus puzzles to uncover words and phrases associated with this holiday.

sp +  +

l +  + **s**

_____

 − **cube** +

 + **c** +

_____

 − **p** + **d** +

 − **ink** + **d** +

 − **f**

_____

 +

− **lemon** +

s +

_____

Family Fun Times

Name _____

On the Fourth of July, families across the U.S. are getting together for fun and celebration. Find out what each family below is doing. Draw a line through the three words in a row that belong together. Write on the line the name of the activity or location from the Word Bank.

Word Bank

picnic	hiking
camping	beach
zoo	amusement park

Lee Family

_____

drum	campfire	dog
dress	tent	backpack
bathing suit	sleeping bag	dessert

Ruiz Family

_____

water	sand	shells
fan	cat	TV
pillow	purse	shoes

Wallace Family

_____

basket	swing	grass
table	roller coaster	games
food	monkeys	sister

Goldfarb Family

_____

flowers	pail	feeding time
rides	lions	roller coaster
cage	candy	music

Play tic-tac-toe with categories. Draw a large gameboard. Determine a category. Take turns writing words in the spaces. The first person to write three words in a row—across, down, or diagonally—is the winner.

Twelve Months in a Year

Name _____

THE NAMES OF THE MONTHS ALL HAVE ROMAN ORIGINS! DID YOU THINK SOMEBODY JUST MADE 'EM UP?

Try this brain teaser. Each equation listed below contains numbers and initials that will form a factual phrase. For example, the title of this page would be written 12 M in a Y.

1. 12 D of C
    _____

2. 26 L in the A
    _____

3. 7 D of K
    _____

4. 366 D in a LY
    _____

5. 103 P aboard the M
    _____

6. 551 F, the H of the S of L
    _____

7. 50 S in the USA
    _____

8. 3 F in a Y
    _____

9. 100 P in a D
    _____

10. 12 I in a F
    _____

Have a Ball!

Name _____

There's nothing better than a game of baseball on a summer day. How well do you know your baseball terms? Count the strings on each baseball. Write the amount on each baseball. Then use the letters above and below the baseball to break the code.

H  **W**

E **O** **K** **B** **L**
T **I** **F** **S** **Y**

A (ball)
G

n (ball)
P

1. $\underline{5}\ \overline{1}\ \underline{5}\ \overline{4}\quad \overline{7}\ \overline{10}\quad \overline{5}\ \overline{1}\ \overline{8}\ \overline{8}\ \underline{5}$ _____

2. $\underline{10}\ \underline{7}\ \underline{4}\ \underline{9}\ \overline{3}\ \overline{4}\ \overline{9}$ _____

3. $\underline{7}\ \overline{10}\ \underline{4}\ \overline{4}\ \overline{10}\ \underline{4}\ \underline{7}\ \overline{7}\ \overline{10}\ \overline{1}\ \overline{8}$
   $\underline{3}\ \overline{1}\ \overline{8}\ \overline{2}$ _____

4. $\overline{3}\ \overline{7}\ \underline{6}\ \overline{4}\quad \overline{10}\ \overline{8}\ \overline{1}\ \underline{4}\ \overline{4}$ _____

5. $\overline{4}\ \overline{0}\ \underline{4}\ \overline{9}\ \overline{1}\quad \underline{7}\ \overline{10}\ \overline{10}\ \underline{7}\ \overline{10}\ \underline{1}\ \underline{5}$ _____

6. $\overline{9}\ \underline{11}\ \overline{10}\ \underline{5}\quad \overline{5}\ \overline{1}\ \underline{4}\ \underline{4}\ \overline{4}\ \overline{11}\quad \underline{7}\ \overline{10}$ _____

7. $\underline{5}\ \underline{4}\ \overline{9}\ \underline{7}\ \overline{2}\ \overline{4}\ \overline{7}\ \underline{11}\ \underline{4}$ _____

8. $\overline{11}\ \underline{7}\ \overline{1}\ \underline{6}\ \overline{7}\ \overline{10}\ \overline{11}$ _____

9. $\overline{11}\ \underline{11}\ \underline{1}\ \overline{7}\ \underline{11}\ \underline{4}$ _____

10. $\underline{6}\ \overline{1}\ \underline{0}\ \overline{7}\ \overline{9}\quad \overline{8}\ \overline{4}\ \overline{1}\ \underline{1}\ \underline{11}\ \overline{4}$ _____

11. $\underline{10}\ \overline{7}\ \underline{5}\ \underline{7}\ \underline{4}\ \underline{7}\ \overline{7}\ \overline{10}\ \underline{5}$ _____

12. $\overline{7}\ \underline{11}\ \underline{4}\ \underline{2}\ \underline{7}\ \overline{4}\ \overline{8}\ \overline{11}\ \overline{4}\ \overline{9}$ _____

13. $\overline{9}\ \overline{1}\ \underline{4}\ \underline{9}\ \overline{3}\ \overline{4}\ \overline{9}$ _____

14. $\overline{9}\ \overline{7}\ \overline{7}\ \overline{2}\ \underline{7}\ \overline{4}$ _____

15. $\underline{3}\ \overline{7}\ \overline{9}\ \overline{8}\ \overline{11}\quad \underline{5}\ \overline{4}\ \overline{9}\ \underline{7}\ \overline{4}\ \underline{5}$ _____

16. $\underline{11}\ \overline{10}\ \underline{7}\ \underline{2}\ \overline{7}\ \overline{9}\ \underline{6}\ \underline{5}$ _____

17. $\underline{10}\ \overline{4}\ \overline{10}\ \overline{10}\ \overline{1}\ \overline{10}\ \underline{4}$ _____

18. $\underline{4}\ \overline{4}\ \overline{1}\ \underline{6}\ \underline{6}\ \overline{1}\ \underline{4}\ \overline{4}\ \underline{5}$ _____

19. $\overline{3}\ \overline{7}\ \underline{6}\ \overline{4}\quad \overline{9}\ \underline{11}\ \overline{10}$ _____

V (ball) **M**
D (ball) **u**
X (ball) **J**
R (ball) **C**

Rebus Riddle

name _____

August is the perfect time for a picnic. Hot summer days and refreshing drinks go hand-in-hand. Read the rebus puzzles to discover a riddle and its answer.

Riddle: __ __ __ __ __   __ __ __ __   __ __ __ __ __

__ __ __   __ __ __ __ __ __ **?**

 **+ d +**  **+**

dr +  **+**  **– m +**

 **– le +**  **– er ?**

Answer:

cr +  **+ a +**  **+**  **– l**

__ __ __ __ __ __ __ - __ - __ __ __

IF8727 *Challenge Your Mind*

Sun and Fun

name _____

Family Day

The second Sunday in August is Family Day and a perfect time for families to enjoy picnics. Add a straight line to each letter below to create a list of summer picnic words.

1. ⊢∨⌐⌐⌐

2. ⊢⊓⌐⌐⌐⌐∨⌐⌐⌐

3. ⌐⌐⌐⌐⌐

4. ⌐⌐∧⌐⌐⌐⌐⌐⌐

5. ⌐⌐⌐⌐⌐⌐⌐⌐

6. ⌐⌐∧⌐⌐⌐⌐⌐

7. ⌐∨∧⌐∧⌐∧⌐⌐⌐⌐

8. ⌐∧∧⌐∨⌐⌐⌐⌐⌐⌐⌐

AUGUST IS NAMED AFTER AUGUSTUS, THE FIRST ROMAN EMPEROR! PASS THE MUSTARD!

IF8727 *Challenge Your Mind*

"According to Hoyle"

name _____

On August 29 we remember Edmond Hoyle. He lived in London during the early 1700s, and for many years gave instructions in the playing of games. Celebrate the day by solving this wordsearch about fun and games.

C	R	A	Z	Y	E	I	G	H	T	S	O	C	C	E	R	C	E	B
O	N	R	M	I	N	I	G	O	L	F	S	H	P	X	O	O	C	O
M	I	C	H	E	C	K	E	R	S	S	S	O	L	A	L	M	E	A
P	W	H	O	C	K	E	Y	J	E	I	R	L	T	L	L	P	I	R
U	T	E	A	M	S	L	K	H	F	P	A	S	F	R	E	E	P	D
T	R	R	S	V	O	C	C	O	M	B	G	U	B	G	R	T	V	G
E	I	Y	E	O	U	M	G	U	T	K	N	T	A	N	B	I	I	A
R	V	L	L	T	X	J	E	F	M	I	R	S	I	L	T	D	M	
G	I	L	U	L	B	I	K	I	N	G	C	C	K	M	A	I	E	E
A	A	A	R	E	C	S	P	O	R	T	A	O	T	M	D	O	O	S
M	T	R	S	Y	A	C	W	A	T	E	R	S	K	I	I	N	G	I
E	S	E	L	B	R	A	M	Y	T	E	F	A	S	W	N	J	A	N
S	E	L	L	A	B	E	S	A	B	L	L	I	K	S	G	C	M	N
C	H	A	L	L	E	N	G	E	T	I	C	T	A	C	T	O	E	E
O	F	X	O	L	I	D	I	C	E	R	I	A	T	I	L	O	S	T

Word Box

chess	soccer	relax	videogames	roller blading	competition
teams	baseball	fun	jumprope	swimming	computer
dice	volleyball	win	crazy eights	racing	games
luck	basketball	piece	go fish	tic-tac-toe	trivia
rules	biking	archery	mini golf	solitaire	marbles
sport	waterskiing	checkers	tennis	net	hockey
safety	challenge	skill	rally	board games	

IF8727 *Challenge Your Mind*

Summer Scramble

Name _____

There's nothing like a little word play on a hot summer day. See how many words you can make from the letters in the scrambled word. Then use all the scrambled letters to make a word that tells who would rather work with numbers than words. Write your answer above the score box.

I N T M A C I T S E A H A M

2-letter words

_____ _____
_____ _____
_____ _____
_____ _____
_____ _____
_____ _____

3-letter words

_____ _____
_____ _____
_____ _____
_____ _____
_____ _____
_____ _____

4-letter words

_____ _____
_____ _____
_____ _____
_____ _____
_____ _____

5-letter words

_____ _____
_____ _____
_____ _____
_____ _____
_____ _____

6 or more-letter words

_____ _____
_____ _____
_____ _____

Answer: _____

S	0–10 words—Just playing around
C	11–15 words—Still pretty cool
O	16–20 words—Getting warm
R	21–30 words—Turn on the fan!
E	31 or more—Hot stuff!

Career Capers

Name _____

Labor
Day

In 1894, President Cleveland signed a bill declaring the first Monday in November to be called Labor Day in honor of American workers.

GROVER CLEVELAND IS THE ONLY U.S. PRESIDENT TO SERVE TWO NON-CONSECUTIVE TERMS OF OFFICE!

Unscramble the letters below to identify each description given. Which work sounds most interesting to you? _____

Description	Scrambled Letters	Job
1. makes, finishes, and repairs wooden structures	p n r t e a r c e	_____
2. designs structures, machines, and systems	n i e n e g r e	_____
3. provides medical treatment	o t r c d o	_____
4. repairs machines, vehicles, or tools	i n a c m e h c	_____
5. transmits messages over the air	r o b d c t r s a e a	_____
6. studies forms of life from prehistoric times	o t o l a e n i g o t l p s	_____
7. hears and decides cases in a court of law	e g u j d	_____
8. creates with words	h o t u a r	_____
9. keeps and checks financial records	t a o u c n c n t a	_____
10. provides medical care to animals	n r a n r e t v e i a i	_____

September...
Remember?

name _____

It's September. Time to sharpen your memory skills. Fold back the bottom half of this paper. Then study the picture for 3-5 minutes. Flip your paper and answer the questions. Open to the picture to see how you did.

1. What time is it? _____ What is the room number? _____

2. How many student desks? _____

3. What is the weather like?
   _____

4. What is on the file cabinet?
   _____

5. Who is the teacher?
   _____

6. What is under the windows?
   _____

7. What math problem is on the chalkboard? _____

8. How many windows are in the door? _____

9. How many chalkboard erasers?
   _____

10. How many drawers are in the file cabinet? _____ .

11. What is between the windows and the chalkboard? _____

12. What word is above the windows?
    _____

13. Where is the flag?
    _____

14. What is in the southwest corner?
    _____

Hidden, No "Kidden"

name _____

The words in the schoolhouse are hidden in these sentences. They may be found in the middle of a word or by combining the end of one word with the beginning of the next. Highlight each word found. The first one is done for you.

1. Would you like more tea, Cheryl?

2. "Open cilantro for flavoring," suggested the chef.

3. Mark, erase the boards, please.

4. Skid slowly on soft ice.

5. Your program does not compute, Rachael.

6. Nab oysters from the shells on Nantucket Island.

7. "Move the llama, then the zebra," ordered the director of the San Diego Zoo.

8. Clap, please, after the dance recital.

9. Ziggy, my favorite cartoon character, is bald.

10. When is the Valentine's Day party?

11. The Olympian figure skater made skating look easy.

12. The label looked like that in a J.C. Penney shirt.

13. Was Allegra destroyed by criticism?

14. Pa, in tse-tse flies, are there stingers that cause sleeping sickness?

15. My pa, personally, is the best dad in the world.

16. My instructor always reminds me to think before I act.

17. The past encourages the future.

18. The orchestra includes a viola, bass, and violins.

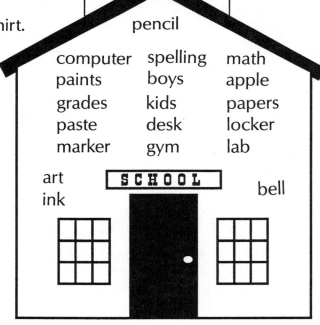

pencil

computer	spelling	math
paints	boys	apple
grades	kids	papers
paste	desk	locker
marker	gym	lab

art
ink

SCHOOL

bell

IF8727 *Challenge Your Mind*

Patriotic Papers

Name _____

On September 8 and September 17, Americans honor the two documents important to the country's history. Discover some facts about these patriotic papers by supplying the vowels which time and aging have eroded.

1. Sptmbr 8 s Ntnl Pldg f llgnc Dy. _____

    _____

2. Kds frst rctd th pldg s thy sltd th flg n 1892.

    _____

3. n 1954, th wrds "ndr Gd" wr ddd.

    _____

4. Sptmbr 17 s th nnvrsry f th sgnng f th Cnstttn f th ntd stts.

    _____

    _____

5. Ths dcmnt sts frth th lws f th cntry nd th rgts f th ppl.

    _____

    _____

6. Th sgnng tk plc t ndpndnc Hll n Phldlph, Pnnslvn, n 1787.

    _____

    _____

7. Jms Mdsn ws clld th "Fthr f th Cnstttn," bt Gvrnr Mrrs ctly wrt t.

    _____

    _____

8. Th rgnl Cnstttn s dsplyd n th Ntnl rchvs Bldng n Wshngtn, D.C.

    _____

    _____

State Names

Name _____

Don't be puzzled by these Indian names. Can you identify them as state names?
First write the name of the state by each Indian name. Then draw the matching symbol
of that state on the United States map where it belongs.

★ Ute _____   ☒ Dakotas _____

◎ Emissourita _____   🌽 Alakshak _____

△ Wishdonsing _____   🍃 Arizonac _____

✈ Mishigamaw _____   ⌁ Minisota _____

☆ Massaadchueset _____   ⬭ Iliniwek _____

▲ Misisipi _____   ≈ Arkansaw _____

⌂ Oheo _____   ● Alibamu _____

⌒ Idaho _____   ◇ Tanasi _____

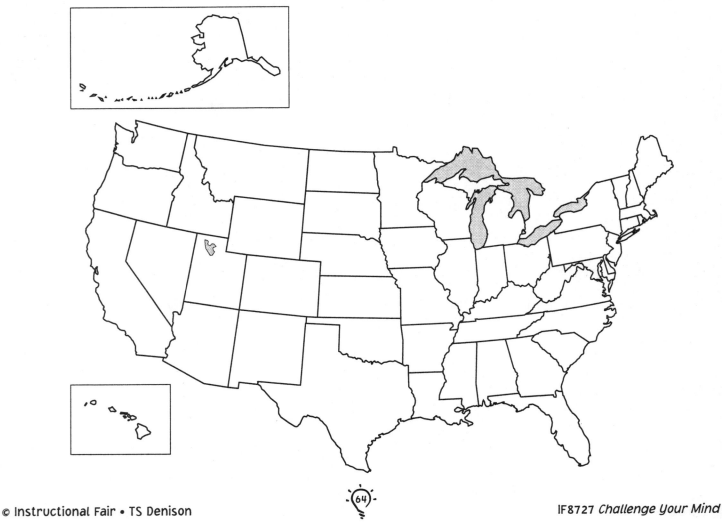

Football Fame Frames

Name _____

Fall Sport

It's a forward pass (horizontal, vertical, or diagonal) into the Wordsearch Hall of Fame. Block the football words found on the locker room wall.

T	Y	A	R	D	L	I	N	E	R	E	T	N	E	C	P	Q	B	U	I	W	C
V	K	C	A	E	I	E	L	D	D	U	H	E	L	M	E	T	L	N	T	I	L
K	C	O	F	F	E	N	S	E	A	K	P	E	M	N	V	S	O	W	N	D	I
C	A	A	D	E	K	P	I	B	G	O	A	L	P	O	S	T	C	O	O	E	P
A	B	C	O	N	C	P	D	I	Z	T	E	A	M	W	O	R	K	D	I	R	P
B	R	H	O	S	M	I	E	L	S	O	V	U	P	L	K	T	C	H	T	E	I
G	E	C	B	E	N	G	L	C	Q	T	I	S	L	M	I	A	G	C	P	C	N
N	T	E	O	F	F	S	I	D	E	D	S	A	T	Y	T	I	U	U	E	E	G
I	R	E	W	E	T	K	N	X	A	A	B	K	U	E	N	L	A	O	C	I	Y
N	A	R	L	J	X	I	E	T	P	T	J	C	O	S	U	B	R	T	R	V	T
N	U	E	M	S	R	N	S	H	O	U	L	D	E	R	P	A	D	S	E	E	L
U	Q	F	I	E	L	D	G	O	A	L	T	O	M	E	I	C	B	U	T	R	A
R	O	E	F	T	P	F	F	O	K	C	I	K	I	J	M	K	I	P	N	I	N
S	C	R	I	M	M	A	G	E	M	V	I	C	T	O	R	Y	C	E	I	P	E
S	K	O	O	B	Y	A	L	P	G	R	I	D	I	R	O	N	L	R	Q	V	P

Word Bank

pass	center	guard
punt	scrimmage	defense
helmet	clipping	offense
stadium	sidelines	offside
field goal	yard line	kickoff
referee	goal post	timeout
coach	gridiron	playbook
penalty	wide receiver	teamwork
running back	touchdown	pigskin
jersey	huddle	cleats
football	shoulder pads	block
quarterback	interception	
tailback	victory	

Bonus

There are two more hidden words that describe the championship all pro football players aim for. Find them and list them here:

The _____ _____

© Instructional Fair • TS Denison

IF8727 *Challenge Your Mind*

Sing a Song of Apples

name _____

Johnny
Appleseed's
Birthday

John Chapman, born on September 26, 1774, was better known as Johnny Appleseed. Number the apple words in alphabetical order. Then write the words in the matching blanks to finish this song to honor Johnny. (Tune: Bicycle Built for Two.)

__ blossoms   __ nature   __ near
__ snack   __ crunchy   __ Jonathan
__ day   __ brush   __ name
__ Winesap   __ loved   __ mother
__ fame   __ tasted   __ wasted
__ king   __ fruits   __ eat
__ appleseeds

Johnny, Johnny Appleseed was his _____ ,
                                        13

Planting _____ awarded him much _____ ,
              1   7

The appleseeds once were _____ ,
                                18

'Til Johnny's apples were _____ .
                                17

Then far and _____ , through the land he "_____" so dear,
                    15   11

Apple _____ were everywhere.
            2

Apples, apples, the _____ of _____ they say,
                            10   8

Apples, apples, _____ one every _____ ,
                        6   5

They're _____ _____ 's toothbrush,
                12   14

So eat one if you can't _____ ,
                                3

A _____ , _____ or McIntosh,
        9   19

They're a _____ _____ , by gosh!
                  4   16

© Instructional Fair • TS Denison

66

IF8727 *Challenge Your Mind*

Cool School Tools

Name _____

It's time to load your backpack and head back to school. Be sure you have all your school supplies. Decode to find out what you might need.

A	B	C		J•	K•	L•		S		W•
D	E	F		M•	N•	O•		T ✕ U		X• ✕ •Y
G	H	I		P•	Q•	R•		V		Z

1. [coded symbols] — eraser

_____

2. [coded symbols] — ruler

_____

3. [coded symbols]

_____

4. [coded symbols]

_____

5. [coded symbols]

_____

6. [coded symbols]

_____

7. [coded symbols]

_____

8. [coded symbols]

_____

9. [coded symbols]

_____

10. [coded symbols]
    [coded symbols]

_____

11. [coded symbols]

_____

12. [coded symbols]

_____

13. [coded symbols]

_____

14. [coded symbols]

_____

IF8727 *Challenge Your Mind*

8 Is Great!

Name _____

The origin of the word October is from the Latin word *Octobris*, which means eight. Many other words begin with the prefix "Oct". Use each definition to help you unscramble the words.

Meaning

1. goatnoc   _____   8-sided polygon

2. toect   _____   8 lines of poetry

3. stopocu   _____   carnivorous 8-tentacled mollusk

4. vetoca   _____   8 degrees between 2 musical tones

5. coodpot   _____   8-tentacled mollusk

6. togarneocnai _____   a person between 80 and 90 years old

7. coheatnord _____   8-surfaced polyhedron

8. cotteamer _____   verse with 8 metrical feet

Write the letters of the word *octameter* in the figure 8.

Greetings Neighbor!

Name _____

National
Good Neighbor
Month

On September 23, National Good Neighbor Day, take time to appreciate your neighbors. Discover some words about neighbors and neighborhoods by filling in the blanks with words that explain the clues. The word in the vertical box is the essence of good neighborhoods.

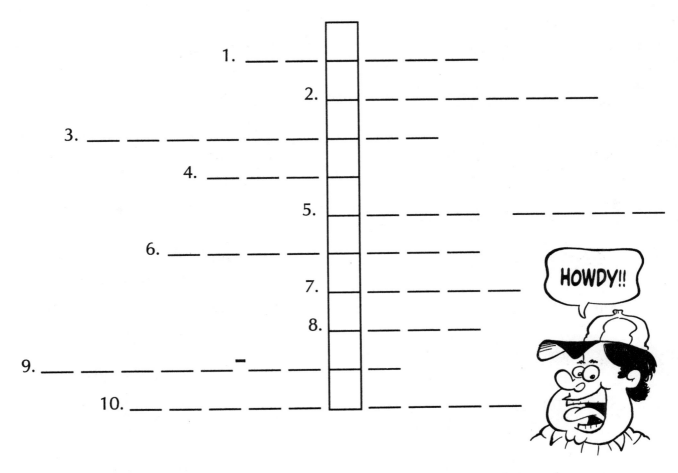

HOWDY!!

1. community watch programs promote _____

2. to show consideration

3. a group with common interests

4. concern for others

5. adjacent houses are _____ _____ to each other

6. youngest members of a neighborhood

7. to loan a possession is to _____

8. offer assistance

9. socially interwoven

10. celebration involving a street full of people

① ☼ ⛭ ⛭ ? ☼ ⛭ ⛭ ? ① ☼ ⛭ ⛭ ? ☼ ⛭ ⛭ ? ①

Good Times!

Name _____

October—
National
Clock
Month

October is National Clock Month, so let the good "times" roll! Decode these timely words by writing the letters from the clocks above the hours. Underlined hours come from Clock II. Then match the definitions by placing the letters of the definitions before the decoded words. The first one has been done for you.

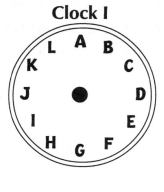

Clock I

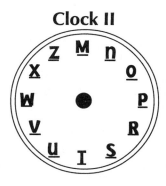

Clock II

__D__ 1. time __K E E P E R__
10 – 4 – 4 – 3 – 4 – 4

____ 2. time _____
1 – 2 – 12 – 1

____ 3. time _____
2 – 12 – 3 – 5 – 7 – 11 – 4

____ 4. time _____
11 – 12 – 3 – 5 – 4

____ 5. time _____
5 – 12 – 8 – 8 – 1 – 6

____ 6. time _____
6 – 12 – 1 – 11 – 4

____ 7. time _____
9 – 12 – 4 – 3

____ 8. time _____
11 – 2 – 1 – 4

____ 9. time _____
5 – 7 – 12 – 4 – 4

___ 10. time _____
12 – 12 – 2 – 7 – 8 – 1 – 4

___ 11. time _____
2 – 11 – 2 – 2 – 10

___ 12. time _____
4 – 10 – 3 – 2 – 5 – 7 – 4 – 4

___ 13. time _____
5 – 4 – 12 – 12 – 4

A. a suspension of time

B. machine that stamps time cards

C. explosive

D. one who records time

E. joint ownership of vacation condo

F. expedient

G. photography term

H. camera technique

I. travel into the past or future

J. artifacts saved for the future

K. given period of time

L. transportation schedule

M. geographical region of like standard times

70

© Instructional Fair • TS Denison

IF8727 *Challenge Your Mind*

Good Grief!

name _____

October 2 is the anniversary of the Peanuts cartoon strip, first appearing in 1950. The creator, Charles Schulz, teaches readers about life through the humorous adventures of Charlie Brown, Linus, Lucy, and lovable Snoopy. Test your Peanuts IQ by completing this crossword puzzle.

Across

1. musican Lucy wants to marry
2. character named after a color, or flower
3. dirtiest member of the Peanuts gang
4. She calls Patty "sir."
5. Lucy charges ____ cents for advice.
6. Snoopy the WWI flying ace fights this character.
7. He carries a security blanket.
8. small yellow bird
9. contents of Charlie Brown's Halloween bag
10. young blonde girl loves Linus
11. Charlie Brown is in love with this _____ girl.

Down

1. Snoopy's desert-dwelling brother
2. Freckled; wears sandals
3. Snoopy was born at _____ _____ Puppy Farm.
4. baseball team's pitcher
5. Lucy's last name
6. Who is Joe Cool?

© Instructional Fair • TS Denison   IF8727 *Challenge Your Mind*

National Pastime

name _____

Baseball Season

The first radio broadcast of a World Series baseball game occurred on October 5, 1921. Print the names of the given baseball teams in ABC order on the lines below. Then write the letters in the circles on the lines at the bottom of the page to decode the message.

1. ◯ __ __ __ __ __

2. __ __ ◯ __ __ __ __

3. __ __ __ __ ◯ __ __ __ — — — —

4. __ ◯ __ __ __ __ __

5. __ ◯ __ __ __ __ __

6. ◯ __ __ __ __

7. ◯ __ __ __ __

8. __ __ __ ◯ __ ◯ __

9. __ __ __

10. __ ◯ __ __ __ __ __

11. __ __ __ ◯ __ __ __ __

12. __ __ __ __ ◯ __ __

13. __ ◯ __ __ __

14. __ __ __ __ ◯ __ __

THE WORLD SERIES BEGAN IN 1903!

Teams

- Marlins
- Padres
- Phillies
- Giants
- Rockies
- Cardinals
- Reds
- Dodgers
- Braves
- Mets
- Astros
- Expos
- Pirates
- Cubs

These teams belong to the:

8^2 10 12 14 5 3 1 8^1 11 13 2 7 4 6

* 8^1 = 1st circled letter 8^2 = 2nd circled letter

Learn Not to Burn

Name _____

Fire Prevention Week is observed the second week in October. Write the letters backward in order to name the most common causes of needless fires.

1. gniyalp htiw sehctam _____

2. dedaolrevo lacirtcele steltuo _____

3. gnikoms ni deb _____

4. gnirots elbammalf sdiuqil raen a ecanruf

    _____

5. gnisu enilosag ot trats eht llirg

    _____

6. gnikooc stnedicca _____

7. gniworht yawa gninrub setteragic

    _____

8. gnirots ylio, ysaerg, ro tniap sgar

    _____

9. ecaps sretaeh oot esolc ot scirbaf

    _____

10. kcabhsalf serif morf elbammalf diuqil semuf

    _____

FIRE SAFETY IS NO ACCIDENT!

IF8727 *Challenge Your Mind*

☖ ☼ ☖ ☖ ? ☼ ☖ ☖ ? ☖ ☼ ☖ ☖ ? ☼ ☖ ☖ ? ☖

Hail, Columbus!

Name _____

October 12, 1492, Christopher Columbus first sighted land. In honor of this event, Columbus Day became a national holiday in 1971. It is celebrated on the second Monday in October. Unscramble the words and write them in the correct blanks to learn more about Columbus.

Columbus was not trying to prove the world was _____ as many believe.
(dorun)
Instead, he wanted to find a shorter _____ to the _____ to build
(teuro)   (lsiend)
greater _____ between the East and the West. After _____ years of
(daret)   (venes)
trying, Columbus finally _____ _____ Ferdinand and Queen Isabella
(dincoevnc)   (gnik)
of Spain to _____ his voyage. They gave him three ships, the _____ ,
(nanefic)   (anin)
the _____ and the _____ _____ . They also provided 90
(paint)   (antsa)   (ramia)
crewmembers, supplies and made him an _____ . He could govern any lands he
(lamidra)
_____ , and could have a share in _____ found and _____
(ridvocsdee)   (utesarers)   (turfeu)
trading. He set sail on August 3, 1492 and land was sighted October 12, 1492. He landed
on an _____ he named San Salvador and called the people there
(daslni)
_____ , mistakenly thinking he had landed in the Indies, near Japan. He made
(sandini)
three more _____ to the New World, opening it to _____ .
(sagyove)   (upornaese)

COLUMBUS, OHIO WAS THE FIRST U.S. CITY PLANNED & BUILT AS A STATE CAPITAL!

© Instructional Fair • TS Denison   74   IF8727 *Challenge Your Mind*

Aardvark to Zebra

Name _____

Noah Webster must have enjoyed words immensely to have written the first American dictionary. Use the clues below to determine the double-letter alphabet words. Write each word in the space provided.

AA = _____ African mammal

BB = _____ synonym for hare or bunny

CC = _____ masked animal with ringed tail

DD = _____ not in sight

EE = _____ fastest land animal

FF = _____ bread cooked inside a turkey

GG = _____ where a yellow yolk is found

HH = _____ to thumb a ride

II = _____ sliding down a snowy slope

LL = _____ the home of a hermit crab

MM = _____ a pounding tool

NN = _____ humorous

OO = _____ a chocolate-chip treat

PP = _____ large water mammal

RR = _____ feeling bad about something you did

SS = _____ across and down clue-type puzzle

TT = _____ a spacecraft that lands like an airplane

UU = _____ a sweeper

ZZ = _____ light rain

NOAH WEBSTER WAS ALSO A FOUNDER OF AMHERST COLLEGE!

Lady Liberty

name _____

The Statue of Liberty was dedicated on October 28, 1886. Celebrate Lady Liberty's birthday by using the coordinate code to discover the facts about this national treasure.

C	R	O	W	n
	J	L	H	
M	W	Y	P	F
T	E	A	R	U
C	X	O	I	B
S	G	Z	V	N
	Q	D	K	

IT WAS COMPLETED IN PARIS IN 1884! SACRÉ BLEU!

1. The statue's real name is "Liberty" R–3, N–5, O–1, W–4, R–5, W–1, C–3, R–3, N–5, W–4, N–5, R–5 _____ the World."

2. It is made of C–4, O–4, W–2, W–2, R–3, W–3 _____ .

3. It was a gift of N–2, W–3, W–4, R–3, N–5, O–6, C–5, W–1, W–4, W–2 _____ from France.

4. The U.S.A. raised $280,000 for the W–2, R–3, O–6, R–3, C–5, C–3, O–3, O–1 _____ on which to place the statue.

5. Her crown has a 25-window O–4, N–4, C–5, R–3, W–3, W–5, O–3, C–3, W–4, O–4, N–5 _____ platform.

6. An R–3, O–1, R–3, W–5, O–3, C–3, O–4, W–3 _____ carries visitors from the pedestal to the foot of the statue.

7. Spiral C–5, C–3, O–3, W–4, W–3, R–2, O–3, O–2, C–5 _____ move people from the base to the crown.

8. R–3, C–2, C–2, O–3   O–1, O–3, O–5, O–3, W–3, N–3, C–5 _____ _____ wrote a poem inscribed on the pedestal in 1903.

9. The poem's most famous line begins R–5, W–4, W–5, R–3   C–2, R–3   O–2, O–4, N–3, W–3   C–3, W–4, W–3, R–3, O–6   O–2, O–4, N–3, W–3   W–2, O–4, O–4, W–3 _____ _____ _____ _____ , _____ _____ .

IF8727 *Challenge Your Mind*

Hiddles (Halloween Riddles)

name _____

Halloween

Hey diddle, hiddle, try these Halloween riddles. To answer the riddles, write the letter that comes alphabetically before each letter listed.

MY FAVORITE DESSERT IS BOO-BERRY PIE!

1. What was the all-ghost baseball team called?

    VIF CPP KBZT _____

2. What is a ghost's favorite dance?

    VIF CVH–B–CPP _____

3. What's green, lies on hamburgers, and has fangs?

    B WBNQJDLMF _____

4. Why was the Egyptian Kid homesick?

    IF NJTTFE IJT NVNNZ _____

5. How did Sammy Spine open his door?

    With a . . . TLFMFUPO LFZ _____

6. What do you call Casper's long-distance calls?

    HIPTV UP HIPTV _____

7. What does a police vampire say?

    GBOH ZPV _____

8. What do you call a ghost who broke his leg?

    B IPCCMJO' HPCMJO _____

9. What is the worst occupation in the world?

    ESBDVMB'T EFOUJTV _____

10. Why was papa ghost uncomfortable?

    Someone put . . . TUBSDI JO IJT TIFFU _____

11. What is a ghost's favorite attraction at amusement parks?

    VIF SPMMFS HIPTUFS _____

IF8727 *Challenge Your Mind*

Spooky Wordsearch

name _____

Halloween

Circle the spooky words in orange and black. (↑, →, ↓, ←, ↙, ↗, ↖, ↘)

V	A	M	P	I	R	E	T	C	S	T	H	G	I	R	F	K	T	R	E	A	T
M	P	U	K	L	J	X	F	A	C	E	P	A	I	N	T	O	O	K	H	C	E
H	A	Q	H	U	Q	R	P	N	B	A	E	M	U	T	S	O	C	W	A	N	M
A	Y	S	E	A	K	P	S	D	M	O	N	S	T	E	R	I	O	E	U	R	V
R	K	P	K	Y	L	N	O	Y	C	W	M	P	X	F	D	R	W	R	N	E	G
V	O	N	Z	E	A	L	X	F	O	E	A	A	M	E	C	B	D	E	T	B	A
E	O	I	S	K	T	N	O	R	G	V	N	R	R	H	A	E	X	W	E	O	B
S	P	K	W	E	S	O	C	W	E	E	S	T	U	N	H	G	U	O	D	T	T
T	S	P	U	Y	N	E	L	S	E	B	I	Y	C	E	A	N	P	L	R	C	A
M	U	M	M	Y	R	P	T	A	B	E	O	F	P	M	N	A	M	F	I	O	E
K	V	U	O	A	O	A	K	M	O	O	N	A	E	R	I	R	O	J	O	K	R
C	I	P	C	S	C	A	R	Y	W	L	I	S	V	I	L	O	O	B	C	E	T
I	M	S	C	R	E	A	M	E	L	Y	S	E	N	O	B	E	R	A	M	C	A
R	E	X	N	M	U	T	U	A	S	K	E	L	E	T	O	N	B	T	N	O	J
T	B	L	A	C	K	Z	F	R	E	V	I	H	S	O	G	H	O	S	T	L	Y

BORIS KARLOFF STARRED IN "THE MUMMY" IN 1932! HIS REAL NAME WAS WILLIAM PLATT!

Word Box

ghostly	pumpkin	scarecrow	cider	fall	shiver
October	monster	fright	harvest	mansion	treat bag
orange	Halloween	candy	treat	cornstalk	face paint
goblin	skeleton	autumn	doughnuts	apples	mummy
scary	bats	vampire	crow	games	werewolf
scream	party	trick	boo	mask	cats
black	owls	costume	haunted	moon	broom
spooky					bones

Hallo-sing!

Name _____

Create a crazy song! Fold this page on the dotted line. While the right side is out of sight, write words in the blanks on the left. Then unfold the page and place your word choices in the song. Sing it to a friend!

1. _____
   relative

2. _____
   noun beginning with a vowel

3. _____
   plural noun

4. _____
   plural noun

5. _____
   plural noun

6. _____
   plural noun

7. _____
   plural noun

8. _____
   plural noun

9. _____
   plural noun

10. _____
    plural noun

11. _____
    plural noun

12. _____
    plural noun

13. _____
    plural noun

On the first day of Halloween, my _____ gave to
                                      1
me an _____ in a dead tree.
        2
On the second day of Halloween, my _____ gave to
                                       1
me _____ and a _____ in a dead tree.
     3   2
On the third day of Halloween, my _____ gave to
                                     1
me _____ and an _____ in a dead tree.
     4   2
On the fourth day of Halloween, my _____ gave to
                                      1
me _____ and an _____ in a dead tree.
     5   2
On the fifth day of Halloween, my _____ gave to
                                     1
me_____ and an _____ in a dead tree.
    6   2
On the sixth day of Halloween, my _____ gave to
                                     1
me_____ and an _____ in a dead tree.
    7   2
On the seventh day of Halloween, my _____ gave to
                                       1
me_____ and an _____ in a dead tree.
    8   2
On the eighth day of Halloween, my _____ gave to
                                      1
me _____ and an _____ in a dead tree.
     9   2
On the ninth day of Halloween, my _____ gave to
                                     1
me _____ and an _____ in a dead tree.
     10   2
On the tenth day of Halloween, my _____ gave to
                                     1
me _____ and an _____ in a dead tree.
     11   2
On the eleventh day of Halloween, my _____ gave
                                        1
to me _____ and an _____ in a dead tree.
        12   2
On the twelfth day of Halloween, my _____ gave to
                                       1
me _____ and an _____ in a dead tree.
     13   2

© Instructional Fair • TS Denison

IF8727 *Challenge Your Mind*

A Halloween BOO–st!   name _____

Give your October a boo-st by learning the language of the ghosts. Each word contains the letters—*boo.*

boom	booboo	boomerang
boogie	booster shot	boot
booth	booster seat	

1. high shoe *boo* ___

2. place to make telephone calls *boo* ___ ___

3. loud noise *boo* ___

4. mistake *boo* ___ ___ ___

5. dance to rock music *boo* ___ ___ ___

6. immunization against disease *boo* ___ ___ ___ ___   ___ ___ ___ ___

7. flat, curved missile that returns *boo* ___ ___ ___ ___ ___ ___

8. high chair for tiny tots *boo* ___ ___ ___ ___   ___ ___ ___

Now fill in the missing letters of these ghostly imaginary words.

boo-ty shop	boo-nana	boo-tique
boo-tiful	boo-quet	boo-ffalo
boo-ribbon		

9. so pretty *boo* ___ ___ ___ ___ ___

10. bunch of flowers *boo* ___ ___ ___ ___

11. First prize award for ghosts *boo* ___ ___ ___ ___ ___ ___

12. Where lady ghosts get their hair done *boo* ___ ___   ___ ___ ___ ___

13. wild ox of the North American plains *boo* ___ ___ ___ ___ ___

14. small, fancy shop *boo* ___ ___ ___ ___ ___

15. long, yellow fruit *boo* ___ ___ ___ ___

Spooky Speakers

Name _____

Halloween

Decipher the message of each Haunted Halloweener. Unscramble the word order and write the sentences on the lines.

1.
like
ghost
on
the
the
writing
board
looked
writing

2.
art
the
room
of
me
there
a
was
picture
in

3.
broom
I
at
the
riding
was
the
party

4.
indeed
himself
bat
a
turn
Dracula
can
into

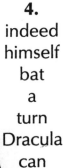

5.
Murdock
werewolf
to
be
Mr.
mysterious
out
turned
the

6.
head
skeleton
of
skull
is
a
the
the

1. _____

_____

_____

2. _____

_____

3. _____

_____

4. _____

_____

5. _____

_____

6. _____

_____

_____

IF8727 *Challenge Your Mind*

Four Heads Are Better Than One

name _____

Mount Rushmore National Memorial was finished on October 31, 1941. Decode the words. Place the corresponding letters of the words in the blanks below to match facts about this famous monument.

CODE BOX

A. _____   _____

B. _____   _____

C. _____

D. _____

E. _____

F. _____   _____

G. _____

H. _____

I. _____

___ 1. America's first president

___ 2. Second head on the mount

___ 3. Substance from which the heads are carved

___ 4. "Tool" used to carve the likenesses

___ 5. Man who designed the memorial

___ 6. 16th American president

___ 7. The mount is part of this range

___ 8. State that houses this memorial

___ 9. President between Jefferson and Lincoln

No ... No ... November

Name _____

Read each clue. Write an answer that contains the letters *no*. Get ready, get set . . . No!

1. the eleventh month

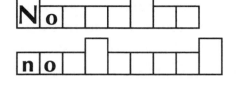

2. animals that sleep during the day and are active at night

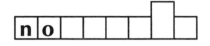

3. to offer as an election candidate

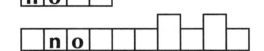

4. a person, place, or thing

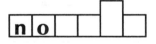

5. a vehicle for snow travel

6. short tube on the end of a hose

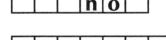

7. has 88 black and white keys

8. study of the ocean

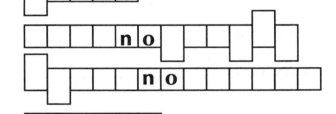

9. king of the dinosaurs

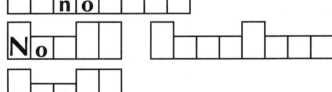

10. small fish often used for bait

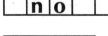

11. single-railed track

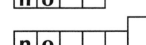

12. state on the east coast of the U.S.

13. a small round hill

14. 12:00 P.M.

15. average, ordinary

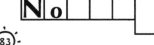

16. star named Polaris

17. a Scandinavian country

© Instructional Fair • TS Denison   -83-   IF8727 *Challenge Your Mind*

I'll Have a "Montagu" with Pickle

Name _____

John Montagu, the Fourth Earl of Sandwich, was born on November 3. When this English nobleman was playing cards, he did not want to stop to eat his meal. He had a servant place meat and cheese between two slices of bread so he could eat with one hand and play cards with the other. He is credited with inventing the "sandwich." Unscramble the names of these "inventors" to see which kind of sandwich they invented. The first one is done for you.

1. Marie Buns _____*submarine*_____

2. G.M.I. Bac _____

3. Toree B. Saf _____

4. Shadee E. Manch _____

5. Doeny Cog _____

6. Shirlee G. Cleed _____

7. F. His _____

8. Chip F. Nerd _____

9. Path I. Kylles _____

10. Lana A. Dust _____

11. Ken C. Hic _____

12. Barbee Cubfee _____

> JOHN MONTAGU HAD A LONG CAREER IN BRITISH POLITICS! YOU WANT FRIES WITH THAT?

Hoops Hero

Name _____

James Naismith's Birthday

Born on November 6, 1861, James Naismith was a gym teacher at a Massachusetts YMCA Training School. He wanted to develop an indoor winter game. So in 1891, using a soccer ball and two peach baskets, he invented the game we now refer to as basketball. Match these NBA teams with their city, state, or region.

____ 1. Supersonics	A. Boston	
____ 2. Jazz	B. Los Angeles	
____ 3. Nuggets	C. Dallas	
____ 4. Bulls	D. Portland	
____ 5. Lakers	E. Seattle	
____ 6. 76ers	F. Houston	
____ 7. Hawks	G. Milwaukee	
____ 8. Bucks	H. Atlanta	
____ 9. Heat	I. Denver	
____ 10. Rockets	J. Phoenix	
____ 11. Suns	K. Utah	
____ 12. Knickerbockers	L. New York	
____ 13. Mavericks	M. Detroit	
____ 14. Pistons	N. Philadelphia	
____ 15. Celtics	O. Miami	
____ 16. Trail Blazers	P. Chicago	
____ 17. Hornets	Q. Orlando	
____ 18. Magic	R. Charlotte	

HE WAS BORN IN ALMONTE, ONTARIO, CANADA!

Cele-BEAR-ties

Name _____

The first Sunday in November is Hug–a–Bear Sunday. Make it a Novem–BEAR to remem–BEAR! Identify these "famous" cele–BEAR–ties using the Code Den coordinates.

Code Den

	B	E	A	R
7	K	F	B	H
6	C	N	P	Q
5	S	V	▨	X
4	J	U	G	D
3	Z	L	▨	M
2	R	W	T	Y
1	A	E	I	O

1. a female aviator   B–1, R–3, E–1, E–3, A–1, B–1   BEAR   R–7, B–1, B–2, A–2

2. 16th U.S. president   B–1, BEAR R–7, B–1, R–3   E–3, A–1, E–6, B–6, R–1, E–3, E–6

3. family of book heros   BEAR E–1, E–6, B–5, A–2, B–1, A–1, E–6 BEAR B–5

4. American Patriot   BEAR B–4, B–1, R–3, A–1, E–6   E–7, B–2, B–1, E–6, B–7, E–3, A–1, E–6

5. WWII flying ace   A–2, R–7, E–1 B–2, E–1, R–4   BEAR R–1, E–6

6. African-American comedian   A–7, A–1, E–3, E–3   B–6 , R–1, B–5 BEAR

7. rock-and-roll king   E–1, E–3, E–5, A–1, B–5   BEAR B–5, E–3, E–1, R–2

8. Tom Sawyer's pal   R–7, E–4, B–6, B–7, E–3, E–1   BEAR R–2, E–7, A–1, E–6, E–6

9. children's author   BEAR E–5, E–1, B–2, E–3, R–2   B–6, E–3, E–1, B–1, B–2, R–2

10. U.S. president   A–2, E–1, R–4, R–4, R–2 BEAR B–2, R–1, R–1, B–5, E–1, E–5, E–1, E–3, A–2

11. scientific genius   B–1, E–3   BEAR A–2   E–1, A–1, E–6, B–5, A–2, E–1, A–1, E–6

12. Red Cross founder   B–6, E–3, B–1, B–2, B–1   BEAR A–2, R–1, E–6

1. _____
2. _____
3. _____
4. _____
5. _____
6. _____

7. _____
8. _____
9. _____
10. _____
11. _____
12. _____

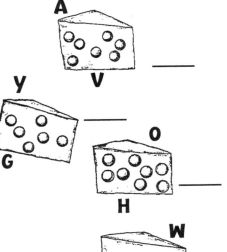

I'm All Ears ...

name _____

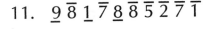

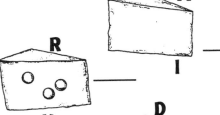

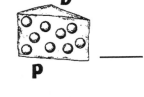

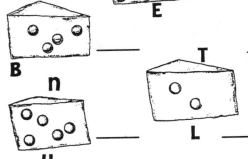

Anniversary
First Animated,
Talking Cartoon

Steamboat Willie, a Walt Disney film, was the first animated talking cartoon. Mickey Mouse debuted in this film on November 18, 1928. Count the holes in Mickey's cheese blocks. Write that number beside the cheese. Then use the letters above and below the cheese to break the code. Example: $\overline{4}$ = M and $\underline{4}$ = B. How many of these Disney movies have you viewed?

1. $2\underline{0}\,\overline{8}\,\overline{5}$ $\underline{3}\,\underline{0}\,\overline{5}\,\underline{6}$ _____

2. $9\underline{0}\,\overline{5}\,\overline{8}\,1\,1\,\underline{8}\,0\,\overline{8}$ _____

3. $4\,\overline{7}\,\overline{4}\,\underline{4}\,\underline{0}$ _____

4. $1\,\underline{0}\,\overline{5}\,\overline{9}\,10\,\overline{3}\,10\,2\,2\,\overline{7}$ _____

5. $\overline{7}\,\underline{2}\,\overline{7}\,\overline{9}\,\overline{9}\,\underline{0}\,\overline{5}$ _____

6. $\underline{4}\,10\,\overline{7}\,\underline{5}\,\overline{2}\,\overline{6}$ $\overline{7}\,\underline{5}\,\overline{9}$ $\overline{2}\,\underline{8}\,10$ $\underline{4}\,\underline{10}\,\overline{7}\,\overline{1}\,\overline{2}$

_____

7. $\underline{2}\,\overline{7}\,\overline{9}\,\overline{6}$ $\overline{7}\,\underline{5}\,\overline{9}$ $\overline{2}\,\underline{8}\,10$ $\overline{2}\,\overline{3}\,\overline{7}\,\underline{4}\,\underline{9}$

_____

8. *101* $\overline{9}\,\overline{7}\,\underline{2}\,\overline{4}\,\overline{7}\,\overline{2}\,\underline{0}\,\overline{8}\,\overline{5}\,\overline{1}$ _____

9. $\overline{10}\,\overline{7}\,\overline{5}\,\overline{2}\,\overline{7}\,\overline{1}\,\underline{0}\,\overline{7}$ _____

10. $\underline{8}\,\underline{10}\,\overline{3}\,\underline{1}\,\underline{5}\,\underline{2}\,\underline{10}\,\overline{1}$ _____

11. $\underline{9}\,\overline{8}\,\underline{1}\,\overline{7}\,\underline{8}\,\overline{8}\,\overline{5}\,\overline{2}\,\overline{7}\,\overline{1}$ _____

12. $\overline{2}\,\underline{8}\,10$ $2\,\underline{0}\,\overline{2}\,\overline{2}\,2\,10$ $\overline{4}\,\underline{10}\,\overline{3}\,\overline{4}\,\overline{7}\,\underline{0}\,\overline{9}$

_____

13. $\overline{1}\,\overline{5}\,\overline{8}\,\underline{0}$ $\overline{0}\,\underline{8}\,\underline{0}\,\overline{2}\,\underline{10}$ $\overline{7}\,\underline{5}\,\overline{9}$ $\overline{2}\,\underline{8}\,10$ $\overline{1}\,\underline{10}\,\overline{7}\,\underline{10}\,\overline{5}$

$\overline{9}\,\overline{0}\,\overline{7}\,3\,\overline{10}\,\overline{1}$ _____

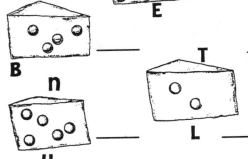

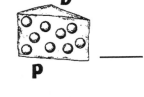

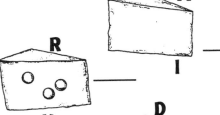

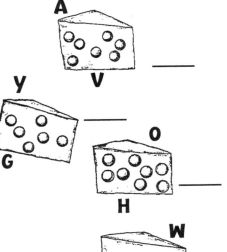

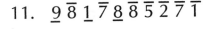

© Instructional Fair • TS Denison

IF8727 *Challenge Your Mind*

Final Grades

Name _____

The grades are recorded but what are the subjects? Use the code to name the subjects studied.

Report Card

Progress Report ___Gretchen Gale___
Name

Grade 4   **Teacher** ___Mr. Crayns___

Grade	Coded Subject	
ß	⌐□⌐⌐⌐•	
ß	∨⌐□••⌐•⌐	
A⁻	□•⌐⌐∧□	
A	•⌐∨□	
A⁻	∨•⌐⌐□• ∨✕⌐□∨	
A⁻	∨⌐□•□□	
A	∨⌐⌐∨⌐•⌐	
A	□□⌐•∨□	

CODE

A	B	C
D	E	F
G	H	I

J•	K•	L•
M•	N•	O•
P•	Q•	R•

S• / T \ •U / V

W• / X• \ •Y / Z•

SAY WHAT?!

Bonjour

name _____

World Hello is celebrated each year on November 21. Learn how to say "hello" in several languages by referring to the code in the box below.

C O D E	A	B	C	D	E	F	G	H	I	J	K	L	M
	14	15	16	17	18	19	20	21	22	23	24	25	26
	N	O	P	Q	R	S	T	U	V	W	X	Y	Z
	1	2	3	4	5	6	7	8	9	10	11	12	13

Chinese   1-22-21-2-10

German   20-8-7-18-1   7-14-20

Greek   12-14-22-6-2-8

Hebrew   6-21-14-25-2-26

Italian   15-2-1   20-22-2-5-1-2

Turkish   14-25-2

Swahili   23-14-26-15-2

Japanese   24-2-1-1-22-16-21-22   10-14

Norwegian   20-2-17   26-2-5-20-14-1

Dutch   20-2-18-17   17-14-20

Spanish   15-8-18-1-2-6   17-22-14-6

Swedish   20-2-17   17-14-20

Czech   17-2-15-5-12   17-18-1

French   15-2-1-23-2-8-5

THE ARTIFICIAL LANGUAGE CALLED ESPERANTO WAS CREATED BY LUDWIG LAZAR ZAMENHOF, A POLISH OPHTHALMOLOGIST!

The First Holiday

name _____

Thanksgiving

On November 26, 1789, President George Washington proclaimed Thanksgiving Day as the first United States holiday. Learn the history of this holiday by filling in the blanks with the words from the turkey feathers.

PLYMOUTH

PUMPKIN

WILD TURKEY

SQUANTO

INDIAN

CAPITOL

BLESSINGS

SURVIVE

SANG SONGS

EAGLE

WAMPANOAG

THANKS

1. _ _ _ _ _ _ _ _ _
2. _ _ _ _ _ _
3. _ _ _ _ _ _
4. _ _ _ _ _
5. _ _ _ _ _ _
6. _ _ _ _ _ _ _
7. _ _ _ _ _ _
8. _ _ _ _ _ _
9. _ _ _ _ _ _
10. _ _ _ _ _ _ _ _ _ _
11. _ _ _ _ _ _ _ _
12. _ _ _ _ _ _ _

1. The first Thanksgiving was in _____ , Massachusetts.

2. It was celebrated as a time to give _____ for their first harvest.

3. 51 Pilgrims and 91 _____ Indians attended.

4. Chief Massasoit was the leader of this _____ tribe.

5. It is uncertain if they ate _____ the first Thanksgiving.

6. The Indian who taught them planting methods was _____.

7. Ben Franklin thought the turkey should replace the _____ as the national bird.

8. In 1972, a flag was flown over the _____ building in Washington, D.C., to honor the Wampanoag Indians.

9. It was hard for the Pilgrims to _____ their first winter.

10. One of the meats they shared was _____!

11. The Pilgrims and Indians played games and _____ for three days.

12. To give thanks for our _____ , we observe Thanksgiving on the fourth Thursday in November.

"Spare the Acts!"

Name _____

Thanksgiving

Trevor Turkey meant to say "Spare the Ax," but he had homonym trouble. Use colored pencils to underline any incorrectly used homonyms in Trevor's letter. Then write the correct spellings above the homonyms.

FROM THE DESK OF

Trevor Turkey

Deer Gourmet Chef,

Eye can't believe it's almost Thanksgiving! I'm sure ewe are looking for knew recipes to try four the big meal. I think aye can help. Hear are a few ideas. Fore appetizers, you could serve celery and karats with dip, sweet and sour meetballs, and sum shrimp cock-tale. For the mane coarse, serve suite potato pi, beats, pumpkin bred, corn on the cobb, and tea-bone stakes. (Notice know turkey?!!!) Owe, and don't forget no meal is complete without an array of delicious desserts. Try serving chocolate moose, straw-bury cheese cake, sour doe bread and jamb, and several peaces of pie. (Remember . . . no turkey!!)

I hope your holiday is fair, not foul—get it? Not foul!!

Your night in feathered armor,

Trevor Turkey

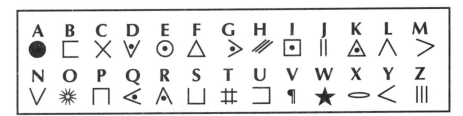

On the Right Track

Name _____

Hunting Season

Harvey Hunter found these turkey tracks in the woods. Were the turkeys playing jokes on him? Crack the code to find out.

A	B	C	D	E	F	G	H	I	J	K	L	M
●	⊏	X	˅	⊙	△	⧐	⫽	⊡	‖	◬	∧	⟩

N	O	P	Q	R	S	T	U	V	W	X	Y	Z
∨	✳	⊓	⪡	⩗	⊔	#	⊐	¶	★	⌒	⟨	⦀

1. Why did the hunter only hunt deer? *They were known to bring in*
   ⊏⊡⧐ ⊏⊐X◬⊔ _____ .

2. What did the hunter call the dried-up river bed? *An* ⊙⌒#⩗⊙⧐⊙
   _____

3. Why did the hunter think the flowers in the woods were lazy? *They were often*
   found ⊡∨ ⊏⊙˅⊔ _____ .

4. What did the hunter call a turkey hit by a bullet? *A* △✳★∧ ⊔⫽✳#
   _____

5. What did the hunter consider to be the highest form of animal life?
   A ⧐⊡⩗●△△⊙ _____

6. What did the hunter call his very own turkey? *A* ⊓⊙⩗⊔✳∨●∧ △✳★∧
   _____

7. How did the hunter define a rooster? *An* ●∧●⩗⧐ X∧⊐X◬
   _____

8. What did the hunter call a gun that shoots slow bullets? *A* ⊔∧✳⧐●∨
   _____

9. Where was the hunter's favorite stamping ground? *The area around the*
   ⊓✳⊔# ✳△△⊡X⊙ _____

10. Why did the hunter take the deer to the taxidermist?
    He really knew ⫽⊡⊔ ⊔#⊐△△ _____ .

© Instructional Fair • TS Denison

92

IF8727 *Challenge Your Mind*

Where Are We Going?

name _____

Create a crazy song! Fold this page on the dotted line. While the right side is out of sight, write words in the blanks on the left. Then unfold the page and place your word choices in the song. Sing it to your friends!

1. _____
   place
2. _____
   celebrity
3. _____
   animal
4. _____
   verb (present tense)
5. _____
   noun
6. _____
   verb (present tense)
7. _____
   body part
8. _____
   body part
9. _____
   verb (present tense)
10. _____
    animal
11. _____
    noun
12. _____
    animal
13. _____
    verb (present tense)
14. _____
    event
15. _____
    food
16. _____
    dessert

USE VIVACIOUS VERBAGE!!

Over the river and through the _____
1

to _____ 's house we go.
2

The _____ knows the way,
3

To _____ the sleigh
4

Through the white and drifted _____.
5

Over the river and through the _____
1

Oh how the wind does _____.
6

It stings the _____
7

And bites the _____
8

As over the ground we _____.
9

Over the river and through the _____
1

Trot fast, my dapple _____.
10

Spring over the _____
11

Like a hunting _____
12

For this is Thanksgiving Day.

Over the river and through the _____
1

Now _____ 's cap I _____.
2   13

Hurrah for the _____ !
14

Is the _____ done?
15

Hurrah for the pumpkin _____ !
16

© Instructional Fair • TS Denison

-93-

IF8727 *Challenge Your Mind*

Ho! Ho! Hoboken!

Name _____

Ho! Ho! Ho!—around the world Santa goes! Discover all the places he'll visit this year. Read the clues and use the Word Box to fill in the letter blanks.

W O R D	**B O X**	Hot Springs Anchorage Hoover Dam	Phoenix Hong Kong Holland	Horseshoe Falls Idaho Houston	White House Hoboken St. Thomas	Honduras Oklahoma Honolulu

1. A New Jersey city on the Hudson River

   HO __ __ __ __ __

2. Alaska's largest city in population

   __ __ __ **HO** __ __ __ __

3. The Netherlands

   HO __ __ __ __ __

4. Peninsula on the southeast coast of China

   HO __ __   __ __ __ __

5. Arizona's capital

   __ **HO** __ __ __ __

6. Central American country

   HO __ __ __ __ __ __

7. A natural wonder in North America

   HO __ __ __ __ __ __ __   __ __ __ __ __

8. Hawaii's capital

   HO __ __ __ __ __ __

9. It generates power on the Colorado River

   HO __ __ __ __   __ __ __

10. The president's residence

    __ __ __ __ __   **HO** __ __ __

11. The state west of Wyoming

    __ __ __ **HO**

12. City southwest of Little Rock, Arkansa noted for thermal springs

    HO __   __ __ __ __ __ __

13. Part of the Virgin Islands

    __ __ .   __ **HO** __ __ __

14. Home of the Astros

    HO __ __ __ __ __ __

15. State north of Texas

    __ __ __ __ **HO** __ __

Homonym Hotel

name _____

The first motel in the United States was opened in December 1925. Read the sentences below. Circle the correct homonym in each sentence and write it in the matching room of the Homonym Hotel.

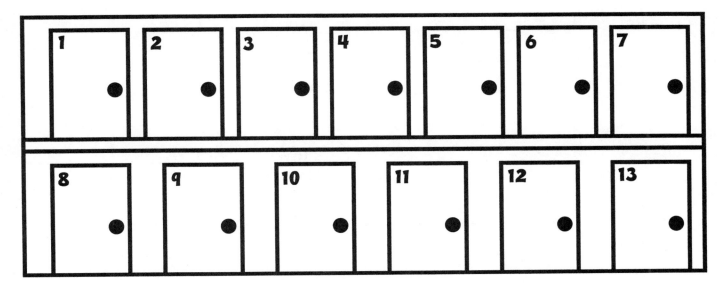

1. We toured an old English (manor, manner).

2. The family went to Virginia (Beech, Beach).

3. The camper's letter began, "(Dear, Deer) Mom and Dad . . ."

4. They visited the (Capital, Capitol) building in Washington, D.C.

5. She (road, rode) the roller coaster four times!

6. (There, Their) minivan had a flat tire.

7. (Meet, Meat) me by the diving board at 3:00.

8. The lion king sat on his royal (thrown, throne).

9. The elephants at the zoo (paste, paced) back and forth.

10. We (new, knew) our vacation would be in August.

11. Have you ever (bin, been) to New York City.

12. Our dinner was prepared in a Japanese (walk, wok).

13. Our (principle, principal) vacationed in Florida.

Daisy, Daisy . . .

Name _____

Walt Disney's Birthday

December 5 is the anniversary of Walt Disney's birthday. Among his cartoon creations was Daisy Duck. To find out what Daisy Duck's father said to the shop clerk on the day of Daisy's wedding, write each group of words in alphabetical order. Then write the correct words in the matching spaces at the bottom of the page.

A. opossum   1. _____
    once   2. _____
    on   3. _____
    otter   4. _____

B. put   1. _____
    purse   2. _____
    pump   3. _____
    puddle   4. _____

C. mask   1. _____
    myself   2. _____
    marble   3. _____
    my   4. _____

D. wrong   1. _____
    wrap   2. _____
    wrote   3. _____
    wrist   4. _____

E. issue   1. _____
    it   2. _____
    inch   3. _____
    innocent   4. _____

F. duty   1. _____
    dusty   2. _____
    dump   3. _____
    "ducks-edo" 4. _____

G. bird   1. _____
    binder   2. _____
    biggest   3. _____
    bill   4. _____

H. my   1. _____
    money   2. _____
    most   3. _____
    Mylar   4. _____

I. plead   1. _____
    plea   2. _____
    please   3. _____
    pleasure   4. _____

WALT DISNEY WON 30 ACADEMY AWARDS! THAT'S A RECORD!

Answer: _____ _____ _____ _____ and
                 I3   D1   H3   F1

_____ _____ _____ _____ _____ .
   B4   E4   A1   C3   G2

IF8727 *Challenge Your Mind*

Hot Line to Claus

name _____

Christmas

	ABC	DEF
1	**2**	**3**
GHI	JKL	MNO
4	**5**	**6**
PRS	TUV	WXY
7	**8**	**9**

Claus has a Christmas *challenge* for you. Use the letters on the phone that correspond to the telephone numbers listed below to see what each person might receive for Christmas. You may have to try different combinations. No calling the operator for help!

1. President Clinton (3 words) 263-9729 _____

2. Tiger Woods (2 words) 465-3833 _____

3. R. L. Stein 786-7437 _____

4. Charles Schultz 732-6887 _____

5. Garth Brooks 484-8277 _____

6. Michael Jordan 763-2537 _____

7. Kristi Yamaguchi (2 words) 423-7465 _____

8. Bugs Bunny 227-7687 _____

9. Tony the Tiger 236-3257 _____

10. Mickey Mouse (2 words) 244-3277 _____

11. Mrs. Claus 266-5437 _____

12. Garfield 527-2462 _____

13. The Bulls 842-8679 _____

14. Sally Ride 227-7853 _____

15. Snoopy (2 words) 364-2663 _____

16. Boxcar Children 222-6673 _____

17. Pinocchio (2 words) 639-6673 _____

18. Dennis the Menace 945-7667 _____

19. Bill Nye 724-3623 _____

20. Snow White 774-6237 _____

IF8727 *Challenge Your Mind*

Candy Canes and Categories

Name _____

Santa's shop is a busy place with food, decorations, music, and lots of gift making. Get in the Christmas spirit. Fill in this chart using words that begin with the letters shown at the top of each column. Write as many words as you can for each box. You may use information sources to help your search. Compare your answers with those of two or three classmates, crossing out any that are the same. See which person has the most original items.

Category	L	I	G	H	T	S
Gift Idea						
Christmas Song Title						
Food						
Decorations						

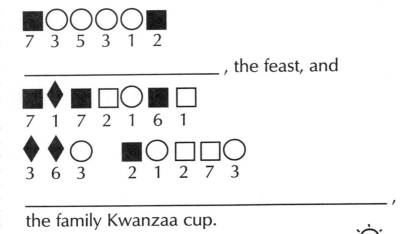

Habari Gani—What Is the News?

Name _____

Kwanzaa

Kwanzaa is celebrated by African-Americans from December 26 to January 1. The word *Kwanzaa* means first. This holiday is a time to celebrate African-American heritage and ancestral values. Discover more of the tradition of the seven days using the code.

Day 1 ■○□□○
       2 1 2 7 3 _____ The day of unity

Day 2 ■■□◆◆◆○○■■◆○
       7 2 7 1 3 6 3 7 2 3 1 3 _____
The day of self-determination

Day 3 ■□◆○○
       2 7 1 1 3 _____ The day of collective work and responsibility

Day 4 ■□○○○○
       2 7 3 1 3 3 _____ The day of cooperative economics

Day 5 ◆◆○
       4 1 3 _____ The day of purpose

Day 6 ■■■○■○
       7 2 2 1 6 3 _____
The day of creativity

Day 7 ◆○○◆◆
       1 1 3 4 1 _____
The day of faith

KWANZAA BEGAN IN 1966!

Traditions include . . .

■○○○○■
7 3 5 3 1 2

_____ , the feast, and

■◆■□○■□
7 1 7 2 1 6 1

◆◆○ ■○□□○
3 6 3   2 1 2 7 3

_____ ,
the family Kwanzaa cup.

	◆	○	■	□
1	I	M	F	E
2	V	T	U	O
3	C	A	L	W
4	n	Z	Q	D
5	///	R	X	///
6	H	Y	B	S
7	P	G	K	J

© Instructional Fair • TS Denison

99

IF8727 *Challenge Your Mind*

Nuttin' for Christmas

Name _____

Create a crazy song! Fold this page on the dotted line. While the right side is out of sight, write the words in the blanks on the left. Then unfold the page and place your word choices on the appropriate lines in the song. Sing the song to a friend.

1. _____ pair of names

2. _____ classmate

3. _____ verb (past tense)

4. _____ verb (past tense)

5. _____ animal

6. _____ noun

7. _____ body part

8. _____ noun

9. _____ verb (past tense)

10. _____ plural noun

11. _____ plural noun

12. _____ adjective

13. _____ adjective

Chorus

I'm gettin' nuttin' for Christmas, _____ are
mad, I'm gettin' nuttin' for Christmas, (1)
Cause I ain't been nuttin' but bad.

I broke a bat on _____'s head. Somebody (2)
snitched on me.

I _____ a frog in sister's bed. Somebody (3)
snitched on me.

I _____ some ink on mommy's rug. Somebody (4)
snitched on me.

I made _____ eat a _____ . (2) (5)
Somebody snitched on me.

I bought some gum with a penny slug. Somebody snitched on me.

Chorus

I put a _____ on teacher's chair, somebody
snitched on me. (6)

I tied a knot in _____ 's _____ , (2) (7)
somebody snitched on me.

I did a dance on mommy's _____ . Somebody (8)
snitched on me.

I _____ a tree and tore my _____ , (9) (10)
somebody snitched on me.

I filled the sugar bowl with _____ . Somebody (11)
snitched on me.

Chorus

Next year I'll be _____ straight, (12)
Next year I'll be good, just wait, I'd start now but it's too
_____ . Somebody snitched on me. (13)

Chorus

Wreck the Halls?

Name _____

Santa's elf, Anthony Antonym, made monstrous mistakes when he posted the Chrismas carol song sheets for this year's festivities. Help him by circling the incorrect word in red or green. Then write the correct antonym on the line. He thanks you "merry, merry much"!

1. *Noisy Night* _____

2. *Oh, Huge Town of Bethlehem* _____

3. *Wreck the Halls* _____

4. *Black Christmas* _____

5. *What Adult Is This?* _____

6. *The Twelve Nights of Christmas* _____

7. *Grouchy Old Saint Nicholas* _____

8. *Gloom to the World* _____

9. *Rudolph, the Red-Tailed Reindeer* _____

10. *Home in a Manger* _____

11. *Santa Claus Is Going to Town* _____

12. *Silent Bells* _____

13. *I'm Getting Something for Christmas* _____

14. *We Three Peasants of Orient Are* _____

15. *It Came Upon a Midnight Smoggy* _____

16. *I Saw Daddy Kissing Santa Claus* _____

17. *Down on the Housetop* _____

18. *I'll Be Gone for Christmas* _____

19. *The Little Drummer Girl* _____

20. *The Last Noel* _____

THE FIRST CROSSWORD PUZZLE APPEARED IN THE NEW YORK WORLD NEWSPAPER DURING THE CHRISTMAS SEASON OF 1913!

IF8727 *Challenge Your Mind*

Wise and Witty

name _____

Benjamin Franklin wrote and published *Poor Richard's Almanac* in December 1732. This book contained proverbs or well-known sayings. Write the letters below in numerical order to complete these proverbs.

1. Early to bed, early to rise, makes a man

   _____ , _____ and _____ .
   L Y A H H T E T E H L A W Y   I S E W
   4 7 3 6 1 5 2 5 2 6 4 3 1 7   2 3 4 1

2. _____ NOT. _____ NOT.
   A T W E S   W A T N
   2 4 1 5 3   1 2 4 3

3. If at first you don't _____ , try, try _____ .
   C U E S C D E   G A N A I
   3 2 6 1 4 7 5   2 1 5 3 4

4. You can't _____ an old _____ new _____ .
   C A T E H   G D O   K R C T I S
   4 3 1 2 5   3 1 2   5 2 4 1 3 6

5. Better _____ than _____ .
   E F A S   Y O R S R
   4 3 2 1   5 2 3 1 4

6. When the _____ _____ , the _____ will _____ .
   A C T S Y A A W   I C M E   Y A L P
   2 1 3 4 4 1 3 2   2 3 1 4   4 3 2 1

7. He who _____ is _____ .
   S E T A H I T S E T O L S
   3 2 7 6 1 4 5 9 8 4 2 1 3

8. One _____ is worth a _____ words.
   C I R E P U T   H U T O D N A S
   3 2 6 7 1 5 4   2 4 1 3 8 7 6 5

9. A _____ in the _____ is worth two in the _____ .
   D I R B   D A H N   S H U B
   4 2 3 1   4 2 1 3   3 4 2 1

BENJAMIN FRANKLIN WAS MADE DEPUTY POSTMASTER GENERAL OF AMERICA IN 1753!

Celebrating Hanukkah

name _____

Hanukkah

The Jewish holiday Hanukkah begins on the 25th day of the Hebrew month of Kislev. Use the clues and the Word Bank to complete the puzzle.

Across

1. This is what the word Hanukkah means.
2. Homes are decorated in this color and blue, the colors of the Jewish flag.
3. The helper candle (servant) of the menorah.
4. What is given each night of Hanukkah.
5. Candelabra with nine candles.
6. Jews pretended to play with the dreidel when these came near.
7. The dreidel's initials, (nun, gimel, heh, shin) stand for "a great _____ happened there."
8. On Hanukkah, Jewish people give thanks for the _____ of their religion.
9. Hanukkah is also called "_____ of Lights."

Word Bank

dreidel	Hanukkah	nine	gods
rabbi	latkes	temple	Shammash
Judaism	dedication	menorahs	festival
white	gift	miracle	Judah Maccabee
soldiers	survival	Jewish	tradition

Down

1. A Jewish top-like toy
2. _____ families celebrate Hanukkah
3. An inherited custom
4. Festival of Lights
5. Number of candles in a menorah
6. Leader of the Jewish soldiers
7. potato pancakes
8. the Jewish religion
9. They fought against worshiping Greek _____ .
10. Jewish house of worship
11. Jewish religious leader

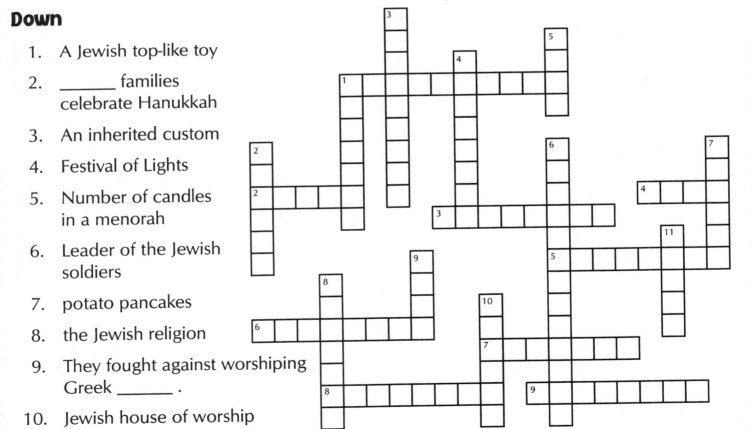

© Instructional Fair • TS Denison

IF8727 *Challenge Your Mind*

Happy New Year!   Name _____

New Year's Day

January 1st is a new year with new challenges. Try this challenge by completing each word that contains "new." The definitions will help you.

1. The youngest infant — NEW B O R N
2. Second part of the Christian Bible — NEW T E S T A M E N T
3. Neighbor of Vermont — NEW H A M P S H I R E
4. Broadcaster of the news — NEW S C A S T E R
5. Recently married — NEW L Y W E D
6. Children's literature award — NEW B E R Y M E D A L
7. Louisiana Mardi Gras city — NEW O R L E A N S
8. American actor — P A U L NEW M A N
9. Fruit-filled cookie — NEW T O N
10. Trenton is this state's capital — NEW J E R S E Y
11. A phase of the earth's satellite — NEW M O O N
12. A small salamander — NEW T
13. He discovered that gravity held the universe together — S I R I S A A C NEW T O N
14. A Canadian province — NEW B R U N S W I C K
15. A short movie of current events — NEW S R E E L
16. One of the Four Corners states — NEW M E X I C O
17. *U.S.A. Today, The Chicago Tribune,* etc. — NEW S P A P E R S
18. The Big Apple — NEW Y O R K
19. January holiday — N E W Y E A R ' S D A Y

List the letters from the boxes above. O T R L O N S U I E
Unscramble to form a word of promise for the New Year.
R E S O L U T I O N

Page 4

Famous Firsts   Name _____

New Year's Day

Celebrate the first day of the new year by researching these famous first facts. Match each word from the Word Bank to its definition. The letter boxes may help you do this more easily.

Word Bank

uno	John Adams	Mercury
Neil Armstrong	Delaware	Jackie Robinson
gold	hologram	Sally Ride
John Hancock	alpha	Green Bay Packers

1. first signer of the Declaration of Independence — John Hancock
2. first state to ratify the constitution — Delaware
3. number one in Spanish — uno
4. first planet from the sun — Mercury
5. first president to live in the White House — John Adams
6. first discovered in California on January 24, 1848 — gold
7. first black major-league baseball player — Jackie Robinson
8. winners of the first Super Bowl — Green Bay Packers
9. first man on the moon — Neil Armstrong
10. Dennis Gabor was first to invent this. — hologram
11. first female American astronaut in space — Sally Ride
12. first letter of the Greek alphabet — alpha

Page 5

Cheer the New Year!   Name _____

New Year's Day

Create a crazy story! Fold this page on the dotted line. While the right side is out of sight, write words in the blanks on the left. Then unfold the page and place your words in the story. Read it to a friend.

1. _____ classmate
2. _____ adjective (superlative)
3. _____ number
4. _____ famous person
5. _____ plural noun
6. _____ plural noun
7. _____ verb (past tense)
8. _____ adjective
9. _____ adjective
10. _____ verb (past tense)
11. _____ verb (past tense)
12. _____ noun
13. _____ noun
14. _____ verb (past tense)
15. _____ adjective

ANSWERS WILL VARY.

My friend _____ and I decided to have the
_____ New Year's party ever! We invited _____
of our classmates, and one celebrity, _____. We
decorated the family room with _____ and
_____. Our special celebrity guest _____ when
he/she saw how cool this party was going to be. We
played _____ music and danced crazy dances. We
snacked on _____ pizza, chips, and pop.

For a special treat, the celebrity _____ and
_____. We were thrilled!

As the midnight hour grew closer, we sat in front of
the big screen _____ and watched the giant
_____ slowly descend in New York City. At 12:00,
we _____ and wished each other a very _____
New Year!

THE ROSE BOWL IS PLAYED ON NEW YEAR'S DAY IN PASADENA, CALIFORNIA! HUT-HUT!!

Page 6

Braille Busters   Name _____

Louis Braille's Birthday

Louis Braille was born on January 4, 1809. His invention of the Braille alphabet made it possible for blind people to read and write. Use the Braille alphabet below to decode these wintry riddles.

A	B	C	D	E	F	G	H	I	J	K	L	M

N	O	P	Q	R	S	T	U	V	W	X	Y	Z

1. What is the jelly jar's favorite month? — Jam-uary
2. What is Adam's favorite holiday? — New Year's Eve
3. What do Eskimos use to stick things together? — I-glue
4. How do you eat evergreen ice cream? — From pine cones
5. What is a liar's favorite month? — Fib-ruary
6. What heavy snowstorm blanketed Emerald City? — The Blizzard of Oz
7. What do you get when your bike freezes? An — Ice-cycle
8. What do Eskimos eat for breakfast? — Snow flakes

Page 7

© Instructional Fair • TS Denison   IF8727 *Challenge Your Mind*

Holiday Happenings

Name _____

Year of Holidays

Find the holidays on the list above the wordsearch. Then write the holidays on the lines below in the order they occur throughout the year.

St. Patrick's Day	Thanksgiving	Independence Day	April Fools' Day
Columbus Day	Memorial Day	Martin L. King Day	Mother's Day
Christmas	Hanukkah	Father's Day	Valentine's Day
Labor Day	New Year's Day	Groundhog Day	Halloween

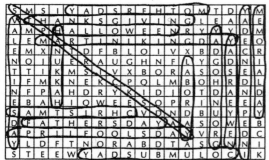

1. New Year's Day
2. Martin L. King Day
3. Groundhog Day
4. Valentine's Day
5. St. Patrick's Day
6. April Fools' Day
7. Mother's Day
8. Memorial Day
9. Father's Day
10. Independence Day
11. Labor Day
12. Columbus Day
13. Halloween
14. Thanksgiving
15. Christmas *could alternate*
16. Hanukkah

Page 8

Duck, Duck . . .

Name _____

Charles Perrault's Birthday

French poet Charles Perrault is best remembered for his *Tales from Mother Goose*. Unscramble the letters to make words that describe these well-known Mother Goose and other story time characters. Write each word.

JUMPY — Humpty Dumpty
M J P U Y

GOLDEN — Goldilocks
D L N E O G

BRAVE — Ramona
R E B A V

VELVETEEN — Rabbit
T E V E V E N L E

DIGGINGEST — Dog
S N I D G I G E T G

LOVABLE — Leo, the Lop
O A E L B V L

ANGRY — Alexander
R G Y N A

SNIFFING — Snoopy
I S F N N F I G

ENORMOUS — Crocodile
N U O O M S E R

"TALES FROM MOTHER GOOSE" WAS FIRST PUBLISHED IN 1697! IT INCLUDED CINDERELLA, SLEEPING BEAUTY AND RED RIDING HOOD!

Page 9

Hail To the Chiefs

Name _____

Inauguration Day - Jan. 20

The squares below contain parts of 18 presidents' names. Match the parts and write the presidents' names on the lines. Cross off the squares as you use them.

velt	Jeff	ter	on	Lin	rd
hower	Mad	I	edy	Eisen	Gar
Kenn	Ad	erson	ison	do	Roose
Fo	solemnly	ington	coln	ton	field
land	Ta	nix	nt	Buren	Cool
Clin	Wash	swear	Bu	Car	idge
Cleve	ft	Van	Gra	ams	sh

THE FIRST INAUGURATION OF A U.S. PRESIDENT TOOK PLACE IN NEW YORK CITY!

Jefferson   Eisenhower   Ford
Lincoln   Coolidge   Van Buren
Washington   Clinton   Carter
Adams   Roosevelt   Bush
Garfield   Madison   Grant
Nixon   Taft   Cleveland
Kennedy

The remaining squares answer this question: *What are the first four words of the presidential oath?* I do solemnly swear

Page 10

Winter Wordsearch

Name _____

Winter Weather

It's a winter wonderland of words. Figure out what words fit the definitions below, then circle the words in the wordsearch. (↑ ↓ → ← ✓ ↘)

Bonus Box
Try to find these words in the wordsearch too:
frost
snowblower
chill factor
crystals
frigid
freezing
sliding
Arctic
snowmobile
ice castles

1. a spike of ice — icicle
2. a large mass of snow sliding down a mountain slope — avalanche
3. a heavy and windy snowstorm — blizzard
4. measure of warm or cold — temperature
5. a heap of snow — drift
6. a bird that can't fly — penguin
7. a house built with blocks of hard snow — igloo
8. small crystals of snow — snowflakes
9. large white animal of the Arctic — polar bear
10. a scoop attached to a handle — shovel
11. used for sliding — sled
12. continent surrounding the South Pole — Antarctica

Page 11

Hot off the Press!   Name _____

Holiday Books

These holiday books sound too good to miss! But you probably won't find them in your school library. See if you can match each book title to its author. The first one is done for you.

Book		Author
A.	*The Littlest Angel*	1. **D** Holly Berry
B.	*New Orleans Magic*	2. **H** Barb E. Q.
C.	*Did the Groundhog See His Shadow?*	3. **C** Howard I. No
D.	*Decorating Tips for Christmas*	4. **F** Spar Klurs
E.	*Crumbly Recipes for Thanksgiving*	5. **K** Mark Downs
F.	*4th of July Is a Blast*	6. **J** Trot Err
G.	*The Voyages of Columbus*	7. **L** Q. T. Pye
H.	*Grilling Out on Labor Day*	8. **R** L. F. 8. Terr
I.	*The Nutcracker Ballet Book*	9. **B** Marty Grah
J.	*Kentucky Derby Losers*	10. **O** Dan D. Lions
K.	*After-Christmas Sales*	11. **A** Minnie Hey Lo
L.	*The New Year's Baby Book*	12. **M** Seamor Shamrocks
M.	*St. Patrick's Field of Clover*	13. **G** I. C. A. Fleet
N.	*Counting the Days 'Til Christmas*	14. **E** Dan Sir
O.	*April Showers Bring May Weeds*	15. **I** Betty Cracker
P.	*My Valentine Love*	16. **Q** Hy I. Q.
Q.	*Smart Kid's Guide to Holidays*	17. **N** Cal Q. Later
R.	*The Ups and Downs of Holidays*	18. **P** Art Throb

"A VISIT FROM ST. NICHOLAS", THE FAMOUS POEM BY CLEMENT C. MOORE, WAS FIRST PUBLISHED IN 1822!

Page 12

Famous Black Americans   Name _____

African American History Month

In 1976, our country began honoring the contributions of Black Americans in the month of February.

Use the clues to fill in the crossword puzzle with the names of famous Black Americans.

MAYA ANGELOU
MARIAN ANDERSON
JACKIE ROBINSON
ROSA PARKS
HANK AARON
HARRIET TUBMAN
ARMSTRONG
GEORGE W CARVER
MARTIN LUTHER KING JR
ARTHUR ASHE

DON'T FORGET JOEL CHANDLER HARRIS!

Across

1. A writer and poet, she was chosen by President Clinton to recite his inaugural poem.
2. Active in the Civil Rights Movement, she refused to give up her bus seat.
3. The first internationally famous trumpet soloist in American jazz. Louis ____
4. A former slave who made more than 300 products from peanuts.
5. The first black to win the Wimbleton Tennis Tournament, he also worked to fight AIDS.

Down:

1. She was the first black to sing with the Metropolitan Opera Company in New York City.
2. The first black professional baseball player.
3. He led the Civil Rights march on Washington.
4. She helped hundreds of slaves escape to freedom on the Underground Railroad.
5. He hit 725 home runs to top Babe Ruth's lifetime record of 714.

Page 13

Famous Duos   Name _____

Valentine's Day

Use the letters on the phone pad to dial these famous pairs.

Example: DIAL = 2 3 1 4

ABC 1	DEF 2	GHI 3
JKL 4	MNO 5	PQR 6
STU 7	VWX 8	YZ 9

MY FAVORITE DUO IS BACON & EGGS!

1. 1 1 7 5 1 5 and 6 5 1 5 1   Batman & Robin
2. 3 1 5 7 2 4 and 3 6 2 7 2 4   Hansel & Gretel
3. 4 1 1 4 and 4 3 4 4   Jack & Jill
4. 4 7 1 9 and 2 2 7 3   Lucy & Desi
5. 4 2 6 5 3 7 and 5 3 7 7 6 3 3 3 9   Kermit & Miss Piggy
6. 1 2 1 7 7 9 and the 1 2 1 7 7   Beauty & the Beast
7. 1 1 4 8 3 5 and 3 5 1 1 2 7   Calvin & Hobbes
8. 5 3 5 5 3 2 and 5 3 1 4 2 9 5 5 7 7 2   Minnie & Mickey Mouse
9. 4 1 2 9 and the 7 6 1 5 6   Lady & the Tramp
10. 7 5 5 5 6 9 and 1 3 1 6 4 3 2 1 6 5 8 5   Snoopy & Charlie Brown

Page 14

Bee My Valentine   Name _____

Valentine's Day

Cross out the homonym in each valentine that is used incorrectly. Then write the correct spelling beside the heart.

Roses are ~~read~~, violets are blue — red
My cup of ~~tee~~ — tea
To ~~sweat~~ me — sweet / for
~~Maid~~ for me! — Made
~~You're~~ dad with love — To
Loves me ~~knot~~ — hot
For my ~~deer~~ friend — dear
~~Would~~ you be mine? — would
My heart ~~beets~~ for you. — beats
~~Bee~~ mine. — Be
The ~~won~~ for me! — One
~~Eye~~ only have eyes for you. — I
I'm crazy about ~~ewe~~ — You

Page 15

IF8727 *Challenge Your Mind*

Heart to Heart

Name _____

Valentine's Day

What comes between these pairs? Use your knowledge to fill in the missing links. You may need to research a few.

1. Mars — **Jupiter** — Saturn
2. Utah — **Nevada** — California
3. XXXIII — **XXXIV** — XXXV
4. computer keyboard C — **V** — B
5. Norway — **Sweden** — Finland
6. touchtone phone #2 — **5** — #8
7. North America — **Central America** — South America
8. earth's crust — **earth's mantle** — earth's core
9. dō (musical scale) — **re** — mi
10. 2nd baseman — **shortstop** — 3rd baseman
11. Central time zone — **Mountain time zone** — Pacific time zone
12. July — **August** — September
13. insect head — **thorax** — insect abdomen
14. British Columbia — **Alberta** — Saskatchewan
15. $1 George Washington — **$5. Abe Lincoln** — $10 Alexander Hamilton
16. Mt. Rushmore Jefferson — **T. Roosevelt** — Lincoln
17. phlanges — **metatarsals** — tarsals (bones of foot)
18. Spanish number *uno* — **dos** — tres

Page 16

Pair 'Em Up

Name _____

Valentine's Day

February is the shortest month of the year, even during Leap Year. Abbreviations are shortened forms of longer words. Match the words in the left column to the abbreviations on the right. Place the correct letter in front of each number. Not every word in the second column will be used.

d 1. street   a. oz.
j 2. doctor   b. Ave.
p 3. post office   c. lb.
f 4. mister   d. St.
n 5. road   e. Wed.
a 6. ounce   f. Mr.
o 7. junior   g. Mt.
b 8. avenue   h. cm
m 9. October   i. ft.
i 10. foot   j. Dr.
e 11. Wednesday   k. pps.
c 12. pound   l. pd.
g 13. mountain   m. Oct.
h 14. centimeter   n. Rd.
     o. Jr.
     p. P.O.

MAYBE YOU COULD RAISE A HERD OF NAUGAS FOR LIKE, Y'KNOW... NAUGAHYDE!

Page 17

Cupid's Capers

Name _____

Valentine's Day

Create a crazy story! Fold this page on the dotted line. While the right side is out of sight, write words in the blanks on the left. Then unfold the page and place your words in the story. Read it to a friend.

ANSWERS WILL VARY.

1. _____ your birthday
2. _____ a feeling
3. _____ adjective
4. _____ noun
5. _____ plural noun
6. _____ classmate–boy
7. _____ classmate–girl
8. _____ future year
9. _____ plural noun
10. _____ verb
11. _____ color
12. _____ color
13. _____ plural noun
14. _____ adjective

Valentine's Day this year will be celebrated on _____. The holiday honors _____. Cupid was the Roman god of _____. He is often pictured as a _____ _____. Cupid carries a curved bow which shoots out _____. If the _____ hit _____ and _____, they will have a crush on each other until _____. If Cupid misses his aim, _____ will fall from the heavens and _____ upon all of the people.

When you write your Valentine cards this year, remember Cupid and his favorite verse.

Roses are _____,
Violets are _____,
Cupid shoots _____,
His Valentines are _____.

CUPID IS ALSO KNOWN AS EROS OR AMOR!

Page 18

Dream Maker

Name _____

Martin Luther King, Jr. Day

Inside the boxes, write the words that fit each shape to complete this story about Martin Luther King, Jr., a famous black American. The Word Bank will help you.

Martin Luther King, Jr., was born in **Atlanta**, Georgia, on **January** 15, 1929. He loved school and was so **intelligent** that he skipped two grades and graduated when he was **fifteen**. He studied to become a **minister** like his father. In 1954, he became pastor of a church in **Montgomery**, **Alabama**. There he worked hard to gain rights for black Americans. In 1956, blacks and whites rode buses **together** in Montgomery, Alabama for the first time. Afterward, President John F. **Kennedy** asked congress to pass civil rights legislation. King gave his **famous** "I-Have-a-Dream" **speech** at the march on **Washington** on August 28, 1963. Although he was **arrested** and people threatened to harm him for his **beliefs**, he continued to preach nonviolence. He wanted a **peaceful** world for all races. He was assassinated in **Memphis**, Tennessee, on April 4, 1968. His birthday was declared a national holiday in 1986.

Word Bank			
Montgomery	intelligent	together	Memphis	Atlanta
Kennedy	famous	arrested	beliefs	speech
January	minister	peaceful	Alabama	fifteen
Washington				

Page 19

IF8727 *Challenge Your Mind*

ABE-GORIES

Name _____

Presidents' Day

Abraham Lincoln was the sixteenth president of the United States. On February 12, 1809, he was born in a log cabin in Kentucky, and he is honored on Presidents' Day. Honor Mr. Lincoln by completing this chart. Write words to fit each category using letters shown at the top of each column. Fill in as many words as you can in each box. You may use information sources to help your search. Then compare your answers to two or three classmates' answers, crossing out any words that are the same. Determine which person has the most items unmarked.

POSSIBILITIES INCLUDE

Category	L	O	G	S
Major U.S. cities	Louisville Lynchburg Los Angeles	Omaha Oakland Oklahoma City	Grand Forks Greensboro	Santa Fe St. Louis San Diego
U.S. States	Louisiana	Oklahoma	Georgia	South Carolina South Dakota
Countries of the World	Libya Lebanon Luxembourg	Oman	Ghana Greece Germany	Spain Sudan South Africa

ABE LINCOLN'S FATHER WAS A SKILLED CARPENTER AND PURCHASED THREE FARMS IN KENTUCKY BEFORE THE LINCOLNS MOVED TO INDIANA!

Page 20

By George

Name _____

Presidents' Day

Fill in the blanks using scrambled choices from the Word Box to learn more about the man who is known in American history as "Father of the Country."

Word Bank

aniriVgi	kabseorhc	yarolvtueinoR
serohs	cithmerita	lpitaca
ndilhcdarngre	nintalptao	gotabni
nitefnico	gihfsni	larneGe
ramoj	seuoH hWtei	ksrworoni

George Washington was born in the state of _Virginia_ . At the age of 3, his family moved to a large _plantation_ called Mt. Vernon. Then when he was seven, the family moved to Ferry Farm close to his father's _ironworks_ . As a schoolboy, George's favorite subject was _arithmetic_ . George had a lifelong love of _horses_ . He enjoyed hunting, _fishing_ , and _boating_ on the river.

In 1752, George decided to join the military. He was commissioned a _major_ and was asked to train other soldiers. Eventually he was given the title of _General_ of the Armies of the United States.

George married a widow named Martha Custis at her Virginia plantation called the _White_ _House_ . Martha and George raised her two children and later raised two _grandchildren_ whose father died during the _Revolutionary_ War.

After two terms as President, George helped plan the new U.S. _capital_ which was named in his honor.

Washington died at age 67 when he got a throat _infection_ after riding _horseback_ in the snow.

Page 21

1-800-Mush

Name _____

Iditarod Race

Fill in the blanks with words from the Word Bank.

Word Bank

transport	Nome	medicines	Anchorage
dog mushing	difficult	life-saving	finish line
Iditarod			diptheria

Every March, a sled dog race takes place in Alaska called the _Iditarod_ . It originated when _dog mushing_ was used to _transport_ vaccines over 1,000 miles of rough terrain. These _medicines_ were needed to fight a disease called _diptheria_ , so their mission was truly a _life-saving_ one. Today's race is in memory of that run. This _difficult_ race is 1,049 miles long. The trip begins in _Anchorage_ , and the dogs cross the _finish line_ on Front Street in _Nome_ , Alaska.

THE HUSKY IS THE SLED DOG OF CHOICE! MUSH!

Page 22

Ask the Doctor

Name _____

Dr. Seuss's Birthday

Born on March 2, 1904 in Springfield, Massachusetts, Dr. Seuss wrote over 50 books for children. Match the clues with the correct titles to fill in the boxes. Then read the highlighted boxes vertically to learn Dr. Seuss' birth name.

Titles List

Fox In Socks	Daisy Head Mayzie
Butter Battle Book	Thidwick the Big-Hearted Moose
Horton Hears a Who	Green Eggs & Ham
Yertle the Turtle	Horton Hatches the Egg
How the Grinch Stole Christmas	Bartholomew & the Oobleck
The Cat in the Hat	The King's Stilts
Boom Boom Boom	King's Beard

1. HORTONHATCHESTHEEGG
2. THECATINTHEHAT
3. YERTLETHETURTLE
4. BARTHOLOMEW&THEOOBLECK
5. DAISYHEADMAYZIE
6. BOOMBOOMBOOM
7. HORTONHEARSAWHO
8. KINGSBEARD
9. THIDWICKTHEBIGHEARTEDMOOSE
10. GREENEGGS&HAM
11. THEKINGSSTILTS
12. FOXINSOCKS
13. HOWTHEGRINCHSTOLECHRISTMAS
14. BUTTERBATTLEBOOK

1. Male produces oval-shaped object
2. feline with headgear
3. shelled animal with rhyming name
4. male with green goop
5. female with floral head
6. loud noises
7. male with auditory gift
8. royalty's whiskers
9. quadruped with large, beating organ
10. grass-colored breakfast food
11. tall walking sticks belonging to royalty
12. carnivorous animal with foot warmers
13. ogre steals December holiday
14. fight of the bread spread

Page 23

The Birthday Bell

Name _____

Alexander Graham Bell's Birthday

Call waiting! Redial! Alexander Graham Bell would be surprised at the changes to the telephone since his invention was patented in March 1876. Use the Touch Tone Code to discover some fun phone facts.
(Example: 2 = C, 2 = A, 2 = B)

Touch Tone Code

1	2 ABC	3 DEF
4 GHI	5 JKL	6 MNO
7 PRS	8 TUV	9 WXY
	0	

1. Alexander's home country was 7 2 6 8 5 2 6 3 . **SCOTLAND**

2. After coming to the United States in 1871, he taught people who were deaf in 2 6 7 8 6 6 . **BOSTON**

3. The invention of the telephone happened quite by 2 2 2 4 3 3 6 8 . **ACCIDENT**

4. Bell spilled 2 2 8 8 3 7 9 2 2 4 3 **BATTERY ACID** on his clothes.

5. He then called, " 6 7 . 9 2 8 7 6 6 , 2 6 6 3 4 3 7 3 . **MR. WATSON, COME HERE** I want you."

6. Watson heard the first actual 8 7 2 6 7 6 4 8 8 3 3 **TRANSMITTED** speech.

7. The first telephone company, 2 3 5 5 8 3 5 3 7 4 6 6 3 2 6 6 7 2 6 9 **BELL TELEPHONE COMPANY** began in July, 1877.

8. Bell filed his patent just a few hours before 3 5 4 7 4 2 4 7 2 9 **ELISHA GRAY** , another American inventor, whom Western Union claimed had invented the telephone first.

Page 24

Mardi Gras Madness

Name _____

Mardi Gras

Create a crazy story! Fold this page on the dotted line. While the right side is out of sight, write words in the blanks on the left. Then unfold the page and place your word choices in the story. Share your creation with a friend.

1. _____ your teacher
2. _____ type of transportation
3. _____ length of time
4. _____ noun
5. _____ classmate
6. _____ adjective
7. _____ number
8. _____ adjective
9. _____ plural noun
10. _____ plural noun
11. _____ adjective
12. _____ plural noun
13. _____ boy classmate
14. _____ verb (past)

ANSWERS WILL VARY.

Our teacher, _____ , took us on a magical Mardi Gras field trip. We traveled by _____ . It took us _____ to get to New Orleans. When we unpacked, I discovered that I had forgotten my _____ , so I had to borrow one from _____ . We stayed in a _____ hotel with _____ floors. Each room had a little balcony overlooking _____ streets where groups of _____ roamed all day and night.

The highlight of our trip was the day of the Mardi Gras parade. People in the parade wore masks made of _____ . Their clothes were very _____ . As the floats passed, the passengers threw us necklaces made of _____ . _____ really looked weird in a necklace! When all of the excitement was over, we walked back to our hotel, where we _____ until 3:00 in the morning! It was a trip we will never forget!

SAY WHAT.....?!

Page 25

Happy Birthday Albert!

Name _____

Albert Einstein's Birthday

Albert Einstein is best remembered as a leading scientific thinker in the field of physics. The anniversary of his birthday is March 14. Today the field of science offers many career opportunities. Use the code box to match the job descriptions with the career titles.

CODE BOX

A	B	C	D	E	F	G	H	I	J	K	L	M
3	26	11	7	4	23	12	14	2	22	16	8	18

N	O	P	Q	R	S	T	U	V	W	X	Y	Z
9	1	15	20	5	19	6	10	25	13	24	17	21

1. I study animal life. **ZOOLOGIST** (21 – 1 – 1 – 8 – 1 – 12 – 2 – 19 – 6)

2. Using our natural resources properly is my main concern. **CONSERVATIONIST** (11 – 1 – 9 – 19 – 4 – 5 – 25 – 3 – 6 – 2 – 1 – 9 – 2 – 19 – 6)

3. I design circuitry. **ELECTRICIAN** (4 – 8 – 4 – 11 – 6 – 5 – 2 – 11 – 2 – 3 – 9)

4. I study plant life. **BOTANIST** (26 – 1 – 6 – 3 – 9 – 2 – 19 – 6)

5. The universe is my area of study. **ASTRONOMER** (3 – 19 – 6 – 5 – 1 – 9 – 1 – 18 – 4 – 5)

6. I study the origin of human beings. **ANTHROPOLOGIST** (3 – 9 – 6 – 14 – 5 – 1 – 15 – 1 – 8 – 1 – 12 – 2 – 19 – 6)

7. I mix different kinds of matter to make new materials. **CHEMIST** (11 – 14 – 4 – 18 – 2 – 19 – 6)

8. I study and forecast weather. **METEOROLOGIST** (18 – 4 – 6 – 4 – 1 – 5 – 1 – 12 – 2 – 19 – 6)

9. Rocks and minerals are my interests. **GEOLOGIST** (12 – 4 – 1 – 8 – 1 – 12 – 2 – 19 – 6)

10. I design machines using heat and power. **MECHANICAL ENGINEER** (18 – 4 – 11 – 14 – 3 – 9 – 2 – 11 – 3 – 8) (4 – 9 – 12 – 2 – 9 – 4 – 4 – 5)

Page 26

McKerry O'Grid, the Leprechaun Kid

Name _____

St. Patrick's Day

Sure 'N Begorra, no St. Patrick's Day would be complete without knowing the language of the leprechauns. Use the grid to decode these Irish words, places, and phrases. The first coordinate given is the horizontal row of numbers. The first word has been done for you.

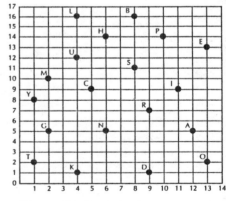

1. **BLARNEY STONE** 8,16 4,16 12,5 9,7 6,5 13,13 1,8 8,11 1,2 13,2 6,5 13,13

2. **SHAMROCK** 8,11 6,14 12,5 2,10 9,7 13,2 8,11 4,1

3. **SHILLELAGH** 8,11 6,14 11,9 4,16 4,16 13,13 4,16 12,5 2,5 6,14

4. **EMERALD ISLE** 13,13 2,10 13,13 13,2 3,13 9,7 1,8 8,11 4,16 13,13

5. **KILLARNEY** 4,1 11,9 4,16 4,16 12,5 9,7 6,5 13,13 1,8

6. **LEPRECHAUN** 4,16 13,13 15,13 5,9 13,13 5,9 6,14 12,5 4,12 6,5

7. **BEGORRA** 8,16 13,13 13,2 9,7 12,5

Page 27

© Instructional Fair • TS Denison

109

IF8727 Challenge Your Mind

March "Tri"umphs
Name _____

St. Patrick's Day

St. Patrick's Day honors the patron saint of Ireland who died on March 17. Many people believe St. Patrick used the shamrock to illustrate the idea of the trinity to Christians. Use the Word Box to help you complete the words beginning with "tri," which means three.

Word Box
tricycle
tripod
trivet   triple   trio
triplets   triple header
triathlon   triple decker
trilogy   triplane   tricep

1. athletic contest with swimming, bicycling, and running events — TRIATHLON
2. singing group of 3 people — TRIO
3. three-legged camera stand — TRIPOD
4. three-base hit in baseball — TRIPLE
5. three-layered sandwich — TRIPLE DECKER
6. three games or events in a row — TRIPLE HEADER
7. three babies born at the same time — TRIPLETS
8. three-legged stand for a hot dish — TRIVET
9. three-headed muscle of the upper arm — TRICEP
10. series of three books on same theme by the same author — TRILOGY
11. three-wheeled bicycle — TRICYCLE
12. airplane with wings above each other in 3 levels — TRIPLANE

Page 28

Wearin' o' the Green
Name _____

St. Patrick's Day

What is your "Green IQ" for March? Use the definitions below to help you identify each one. Have your teacher read the answers. For each correct answer score the number of points shown. Total the points to determine your Green IQ.

1. U.S. paper money nickname — GREEN**BACK** (3)
2. a fir or pine tree — **EVER**GREEN (1)
3. a minty flavor — **WINTER**GREEN (2)
4. a glass-sided building for plant growing — GREEN**HOUSE** (1)
5. ID card for a foreigner with permanent residence in the U.S. — GREEN**CARD** (3)
6. the Prime Meridian passes through it — GREEN**WICH** (2)
7. an inexperienced person — GREEN**HORN** (2)
8. Is the moon really made of this? — GREEN **CHEESE** (1)
9. world's largest island—near Canada — GREEN**LAND** (1)
10. gardening "know how" — GREEN**THUMB** (2)
11. a traffic signal meaning "Go" — GREEN**LIGHT** (1)
12. plants or foliage — GREEN**ERY** (2)
13. jealousy — GREEN**-EYED** (2)
14. special U.S. military forces — GREEN **BERETS** (3)

wintergreen	green card	evergreen	greenery
Greenwich	greenhorn	Greenland	greenback
green cheese	green light	greenhouse	green-eyed
green thumb	Green Berets		

Total Score: _____
A perfect "Green IQ" score totals 26 points.

Page 29

Medieval March
Name _____

March Fun

Become acquainted with the Middle Ages in March. Research the knightly terms to work the puzzle.

Across
1. customs of medieval knighthood
2. King Arthur's sword
3. King Arthur's circular table
4. a knightly martial sport
5. combat on horseback
6. magician of King Arthur's court
7. steel-tipped spear of a knight
8. water-filled trench around a castle
9. a feudal tenant

Down
1. armor bearer for a knight
2. a young boy who desires to become a knight
3. the church seat of the bishop
4. a successful squire becomes one
5. metallic body covering
6. an establishment for monks
7. a medieval brother
8. a symbolic emblem (3 words)
9. a large, fortified building

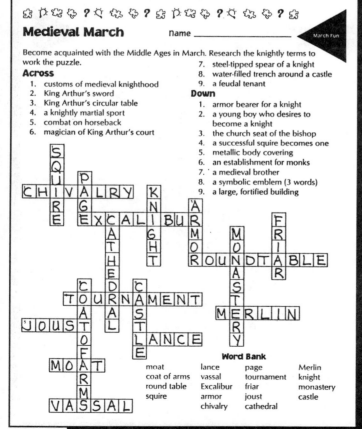

Word Bank
moat, lance, page, Merlin, coat of arms, vassal, tournament, knight, round table, Excalibur, friar, monastery, squire, armor, joust, castle, chivalry, cathedral

Page 30

Don't Be Fooled
Name _____

April Fools' Day

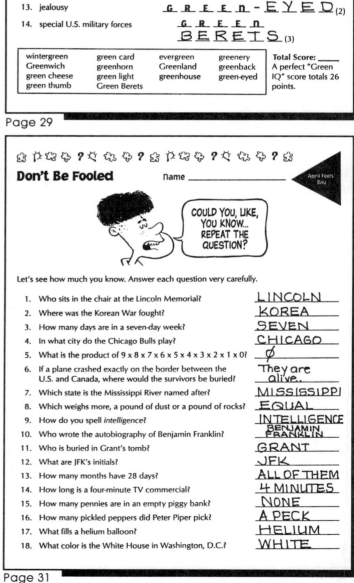

COULD YOU, LIKE, YOU KNOW... REPEAT THE QUESTION?

Let's see how much you know. Answer each question very carefully.

1. Who sits in the chair at the Lincoln Memorial? — LINCOLN
2. Where was the Korean War fought? — KOREA
3. How many days are in a seven-day week? — SEVEN
4. In what city do the Chicago Bulls play? — CHICAGO
5. What is the product of 9 x 8 x 7 x 6 x 5 x 4 x 3 x 2 x 1 x 0? — 0
6. If a plane crashed exactly on the border between the U.S. and Canada, where would the survivors be buried? — They are alive.
7. Which state is the Mississippi River named after? — MISSISSIPPI
8. Which weighs more, a pound of dust or a pound of rocks? — EQUAL
9. How do you spell intelligence? — INTELLIGENCE
10. Who wrote the autobiography of Benjamin Franklin? — BENJAMIN FRANKLIN
11. Who is buried in Grant's tomb? — GRANT
12. What are JFK's initials? — JFK
13. How many months have 28 days? — ALL OF THEM
14. How long is a four-minute TV commercial? — 4 MINUTES
15. How many pennies are in an empty piggy bank? — NONE
16. How many pickled peppers did Peter Piper pick? — A PECK
17. What fills a helium balloon? — HELIUM
18. What color is the White House in Washington, D.C.? — WHITE

Page 31

110

Fools' Day Fun

Name _____

April Fools' Day

An eleven-word phase is hidden in the puzzle below. Unscramble the letters by moving one letter in any direction. You may use each letter only once.

Begin

O L S ' D A Y !
T O F L L A S A
H E F I R S T T
L I R P A F O R
I S S E T A P A

Answer:

THE FIRST OF APRIL IS SET
APART AS ALL FOOLS' DAY.

THE FEAST OF FOOLS WAS A MOCK RELIGIOUS FESTIVAL HELD IN ENGLAND AND FRANCE FROM THE 5TH TO THE 16TH CENTURIES!

Bogus Bloomers

Name _____

April Fools' Day

April gets its name from the Latin word *Aprilis* meaning to open. Flowers often open or bloom in April. Meet the "famous" gardeners who tend these flowers. Unscramble their names to form the real names of flowers. The first one is done for you. Fold back the top of the page and see how many you can solve without the help of the Word Box.

Word Box

aster	poppy	hyacinth	carnation
zinnia	bluebell	petunia	daisies
violet	orchid	daffodil	poinsettia
tulips	sunflower	marigold	

1. Walt Reily — *water lily*
2. Lu Spit — tulips
3. Fil Fodda — daffodil
4. Sue Flowrn — sunflower
5. Vi Tole — violet
6. Cinty Hah — hyacinth
7. Bub Lelel — bluebell
8. Sid Easi — daisies
9. Doc Hir — orchid
10. Stepia Toni — poinsettia
11. Anna Trico — carnation
12. Izi Ann — zinnia
13. Ina Tupe — petunia
14. Marg Oldi — marigold
15. P. P. Poy — poppy
16. St. Ear — aster

SCIENCE FACT NO. 342: IF YOU PLANT SEEDS, STUFF WILL GROW OUT OF THE GROUND!

Are You Stumped?

Name _____

Arbor Day

On Arbor Day, schoolchildren are encouraged to plant trees. This day was first established by Julius Sterling Morton, a Nebraska newspaper publisher, who discovered that trees would enrich and conserve moisture in the soil. A tree-related word is scrambled in each section of the tree stump. Find the letter that is missing from each word. Write that letter in the center. Write the four words below each stump.

Kinds of trees

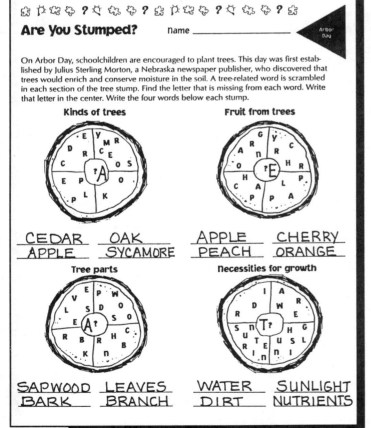

CEDAR   OAK
APPLE   SYCAMORE

Fruit from trees

APPLE   CHERRY
PEACH   ORANGE

Tree parts

SAPWOOD   LEAVES
BARK   BRANCH

Necessities for growth

WATER   SUNLIGHT
DIRT   NUTRIENTS

Seeing Double

Name _____

April–Spring

Bunny rabbits! Spring offers an array of double letters. Use the clues to write a word with double letters.

1. dustlike sparkles — glitter
2. light rain — drizzle
3. soft, airy — fluffy
4. textbook dictionary — glossary
5. to help — assist
6. leaping — hopping
7. brown, sticky syrup — molasses
8. every year — annual
9. red and white striped candy — peppermint
10. tells when guests arrive — doorbell
11. pigskin sport — football
12. rapid repetitive talking — chatter
13. to eat quickly — gobble
14. book pictures — illustrations
15. where you live — address
16. lines that never cross — parallel

Presto!

Name _____

Easter

Abracadabra . . . Oops! When the magician pulled these alphabet strips from his top hat, some of the letters were missing. First write the missing alphabet letters. Then unscramble them to form a word. Do this for each alphabet strip. Fill in the blanks with words from above to answer the riddle.

1.
R	C	Q	G	S	U	I	B	L	V
H	F	K	A	J	X	P	O	D	M

E N T W Y   T W E N T Y
(missing letters)   (word)

2.
Q	H	M	Z	C	I	R	D	X	T	L	S
B	U	F	J	P	Y	G	V	W	K	A	

E N O   O N E
(missing letters)   (word)

HOP TO IT!!

3.
E	J	O	Q	G	V	Z	I	T	C	A
K	R	H	D	P	S	M	X	L	F	W

B N U Y   B U N n Y
(missing letters)   (word)

4.
B	K	O	X	I	D	Q	V	Y	G
H	P	M	C	R	W	Z	J	F	N

A E L S T U   S A L U T E
(missing letters)   (word)

> **How do rabbits honor those who have gone to the "hare"-after?**

With a . . .

1. T W E N T Y - 2. O N E 3. "B U N N Y"
4. S A L U T E

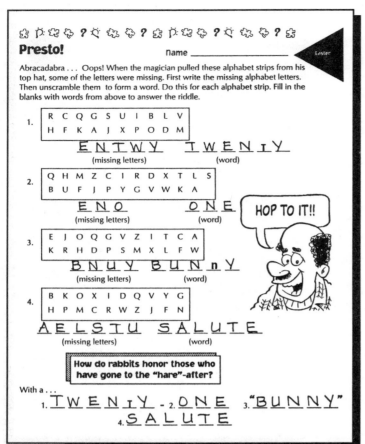

Page 36

Keep Your Bunny Side Up!

Name _____

Easter

Use the Word Box to help you solve these teasers.

1. rabbit wedding march "Hare Comes the Bride"
2. how rabbits order their eggs bunny side up
3. where newly married rabbits go on a bunny moon
4. what bunny nuns wear rabbit habit
5. why Grandma Bunny wore a wig too many gray hares
6. expensive bunny jewelry 14 - carrot gold
7. bunny light green cantaloupe bunny dew melon
8. what deaf bunnies wear haring aid
9. a narrow escape for rabbits hare-raising experience
10. carrots passed down from generation to generation hare-itage
11. rabbit heaven the hare after
12. what bunny cooks must wear hare net
13. rabbit jet travel hare plane
14. James Howe vampire rabbit Bunnicula
15. bunny fur groomer hare dryer
16. a comical hare funny bunny

Word Box		
haring aid	bunny dew melon	14-carrot gold
hare net	hare-raising experience	hare-itage
"Hare Comes the Bride"	bunny side up	funny bunny
too many gray hares	the hare after	Bunnicula
hare dryer	rabbit habit	hare plane
on a bunny moon		

Page 37

Earth First

Name _____

Earth Day

Find the path with a message about the earth. Highlight the message from one side of the puzzle to another.

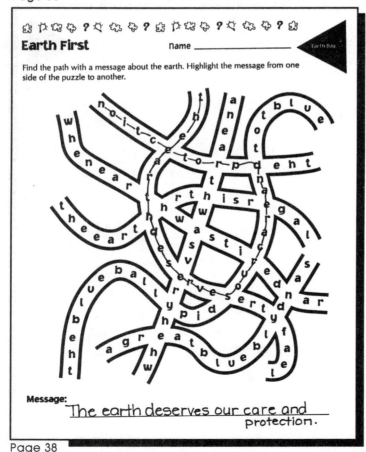

Message: The earth deserves our care and protection.

Page 38

April Firsts

Name _____

Samuel Morse's Birthday

Samuel Morse was born on April 27, 1791 and is best known for developing the first successful electric telegraph. Decode the messages about April events using the Morse Code.

					Morse Code					
A • —	E •	I • •	M — —	Q — — • —	U • • —	Y — • — —
B — • • •	F • • — •	J • — — —	N — •	R • — •	V • • • —	Z — — • •
C — • — •	G — — •	K — • —	O — — —	S • • •	W • — —	
D — • •	H • • • •	L • — • •	P • — — •	T —	X — • • —	

April 2 Juan Ponce de Leon discovered • • — • / • — • • / — — — / • — • / • • / — • • — in 1513. FLORIDA

April 3 In 1860, the • — — • / — — — / — • / • — — •/ • — • • / — — • / • — • / • • • / • • • began. PONY EXPRESS

April 6 In 1896, the first — — — / • — • • / • — — • / — — • • • / • • • / — • — — • / • — / — — / • — • • were held in Athens, Greece. OLYMPICS

April 8 In 1974, • • • • / • — / — • — / • — • — • / • — / • — • / — — — • broke Babe Ruth's record of 714 home runs. HANK AARON

April 14 In 1865, • — / — • • • / •   • • • / • • — • / • — • / — — — / • — • • / — • broke was assassinated. ABE LINCOLN

April 18 In 1775, • — — • / • — / • • — / • • • — / • • • — / — • / • / • — • / • broke made his famous ride. PAUL REVERE

April 24 In 1704, the first American — • / • • — — / • • • / • — — • / • — / • — — • / • broke was regularly published. NEWSPAPER

Page 39

A -May-zing Month

name _____

April! showers brought these May flowers. Use the Word Box to help you write words that have "May" as part of the answer.

Word Box

dismay	Mayas
mayday	mayhem
Mayflower	mayonnaise
mayapple	maybe
maypole	mayor

1. an Indian group of the Yucatan, Honduras, and Guatemala, El Salvador, and Belize — MAY A S

2. American herb of barberry family — MAY A P P L E

3. international radio telephone distress signal — MAY D A Y

4. possibly — MAY B E

5. willful damage or violence — MAY H E M

6. salad dressing — MAY O N N A I S E

7. elected city head — MAY O R

8. flowered pole for dancing around — MAY P O L E

9. sudden loss of courage — D I S MAY

10. the Pilgrims' ship — MAY F L O W E R

I Have My Pride, After All

name _____

The first week in May is "Be Kind to Animals Week." Groups of animals are described with many different words. Use the code in the box below to identify each group of animals. Write the word on the blank.

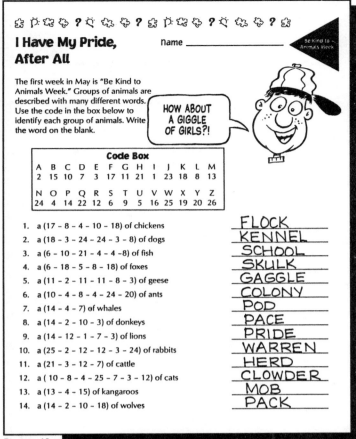

HOW ABOUT A GIGGLE OF GIRLS?!

Code Box

A	B	C	D	E	F	G	H	I	J	K	L	M
2	15	10	7	3	17	11	21	1	23	18	8	13

N	O	P	Q	R	S	T	U	V	W	X	Y	Z
24	4	14	22	12	6	9	5	16	25	19	20	26

1. a (17 – 8 – 4 – 10 – 18) of chickens — FLOCK
2. a (18 – 3 – 24 – 24 – 3 – 8) of dogs — KENNEL
3. a (6 – 10 – 21 – 4 – 4 –8) of fish — SCHOOL
4. a (6 – 18 – 5 – 8 – 18) of foxes — SKULK
5. a (11 – 2 – 11 – 11 – 8 – 3) of geese — GAGGLE
6. a (10 – 4 – 8 – 4 – 24 – 20) of ants — COLONY
7. a (14 – 4 – 7) of whales — POD
8. a (14 – 2 – 10 – 3) of donkeys — PACE
9. a (14 – 12 – 1 – 7 – 3) of lions — PRIDE
10. a (25 – 2 – 12 – 12 – 3 – 24) of rabbits — WARREN
11. a (21 – 3 – 12 – 7) of cattle — HERD
12. a (10 – 8 – 4 – 25 – 7 – 3 – 12) of cats — CLOWDER
13. a (13 – 4 – 15) of kangaroos — MOB
14. a (14 – 2 – 10 – 18) of wolves — PACK

"Cat-chy" Animal Expressions

name _____

Match these animal expressions with their meanings by writing the letters on the blanks.

K	1. crocodile tears	a. pretend to be asleep or dead
F	2. duck	b. a spelling contest
P	3. guinea pig	c. play
B	4. bee	d. to tell on someone
I	5. eager beaver	e. bothers you
D	6. to rat on	f. to go underwater
M	7. hold your horses	g. suspicious
A	8. play possum	h. foolish person
N	9. clam up	i. someone anxious to do something
E	10. get your goat	j. shy, embarrassed
C	11. horse around	k. fake crying
J	12. sheepish	l. terrific
L	13. the cat's meow	m. wait patiently
G	14. fishy	n. be quiet
O	15. a bear	o. something really difficult
H	16. turkey	p. someone who tries something first
Q	17. quick as a rabbit	q. fast

THE FIRST AMERICAN SOCIETY FOR THE PREVENTION OF CRUELTY TO ANIMALS WAS CHARTERED IN NEW YORK IN 1866!

May Daze

name _____

Try to figure out the word or phrase represented by these puzzles. Write answers under each box. The first one is done for you.

1. Strike / Strike / Strike yo u're — three strikes, you're out

2. m ce / m ce / m ce — three blind mice (no i's)

3. 1 — hole in one

4. b b / u / t h / q — bathtub ring

5. weather / cast / cast / cast / cast — weather forecast

6. tire — flat tire

7. FIVE — high five

8. SHOE / SHOE — pair of shoes

9. E L K C U B — buckle up

10. LIPS / Lips — tulips

11. s NUTS — doughnuts

12. ¢ ipede — centipede

13. 2th DK — tooth decay

14. WI NG — broken wing

15. D K I — mixed-up kid

16. S P A C E — outer space

IF8727 *Challenge Your Mind*

Who Said It?

Name _____

1st Comic Strip Appeared in Newspapers May 9, 1897

To identify famous cartoon characters, write the letter of the alphabet that comes after each letter (after **Z** return to **A**). Then cut out a speech bubble and match it with the cartoon character who might have made that comment.

Where are you, Calvin! GNAADR **HOBBES**	*Watch me get Odie!* FZQEHDKC **GARFIELD**	*Mr. Wilson, where are you!* CDMMHR the LDMZBD **DENNIS THE MENACE**
Meet my buddy, Woodstock. RMNNOX **SNOOPY**	*What's up, Doc!* ATFR ATMMX **BUGS BUNNY**	*Nothing ever goes right for me.* YHFFX **ZIGGY**
I'll change in this phone booth. RTODQLZM **SUPERMAN**	*I tawt I taw a puddy tat!* SVDDSX AHQC **TWEETY BIRD**	*I'm "all ears," Minnie.* LHBJDX LNTRD **MICKEY MOUSE**

Page 44

Diamond Dust

Name _____

Baseball Season

Create a crazy story! Fold this page on the dotted line. While the right side is out of sight, write words in the blanks on the left. Then unfold the page and place your word choices on the appropriate lines in the story! Share your creation with a friend.

1. _____ city
2. _____ plural noun
3. _____ classmate
4. _____ noun
5. _____ number
6. _____ two classmates
7. _____ verb (present tense)
8. _____ number
9. _____ body part (plural)
10. _____ city
11. _____ expression
12. _____ adjective
13. _____ dollar amount
14. _____ food item

ANSWERS WILL VARY.

Baseball season is back! This year there's a hot new team called the _____ _____ . Their ace pitcher, _____, has a _____ for an arm. His/her fastball speeds in at _____ miles per hour. In the dugout are two more walking wizards, _____ and _____ . One of them, however, has bad wheels and can only _____ around the base paths. The other throws smoke, often fanning _____ batters in a single inning!

That ball not only has eyes, it has _____ ! And who keeps the batter's box neat? Why, the cleanup hitter, of course. Speaking of hitters, this team's sluggers can hit them clean to _____ . When they do, a roar goes up from the crowd, yelling _____ . So far their season is off to a _____ start, so come on out to see them. Tickets only cost _____ , and there's plenty of _____ to eat.

Lastly, do you know why the rookie had coal on his face? He came from the "miners"!

Play ball!

Page 45

Lest We Forget

Name _____

Memorial Day

Memorial Day is a patriotic holiday celebrated on the last Monday in May to honor our country's citizens who died defending the U.S.A. Number each group of words in alphabetical order. Write the first letter of the number-two word in the matching blank below. The first two are done for you.

1. ★2 enemy / 1 eagle / 3 forge
2. ★2 Marines / 3 party / 1 main
3. 1 united / ★2 weak / 3 weapons
4. ★2 honor / 3 infantry / 1 honest
5. ★2 defend / 3 grave / 1 dedication
6. ★2 parade / 1 Marine / 3 parody
7. 1 glory / ★2 headstone / 3 heard
8. 3 annual / ★2 amnesty / 1 American
9. ★2 monuments / 1 memorial / 3 open
10. 3 Uncle / ★2 treaty / 1 Sam
11. ★2 valor / 1 tactics / 3 veterans
12. 3 yearn / ★2 Yankee / 1 violent
13. ★2 yesterday / 1 peace / 3 youth
14. 1 religion / ★2 respect / 3 soldier
15. 1 stars / ★2 yesteryear / 3 youth
16. 1 salute / ★2 taps / 3 tribute
17. 1 gravestone / 3 nation / ★2 loyalty
18. 1 armed forces / ★2 attack / 3 freedom
19. 1 battle / ★2 enthusiasm / 3 glory
20. 3 bugle / ★2 Arlington Cemetery / 1 air raid
21. 3 tactics / 1 honor / ★2 induction
22. ★2 army / 1 anger / 3 bold
23. 3 forgive / ★2 educate / 1 bravery
24. ★2 epitaph / 1 ceremony / 3 flag
25. ★2 dedicate / 1 decorations / 3 flowers
26. 3 peace / 1 create / ★2 offer

THEY PAVED THE WAY
(10 4 24 16 7 23 15 2 17 3 18 12)

For MEMORIAL DAY
(9 19 14 21 8 17 5 22 13)

Page 46

Palindrome Pals

Name _____

Mother's/Father's Day

During May, we honor Mom on Mother's Day. Father's Day in June praises Pop. The words mom and pop are called palindromes. These words are spelled the same forward and backward. Use the clues to discover more palindromes.

1. a young dog — **PUP**
2. 12:00 P.M. — **NOON**
3. horizontally even — **LEVEL**
4. baby chick's sound — **PEEP**
5. to hang wall covering again — **REPAPER**
6. horn sound — **TOOT**
7. a dipping into water for apples game — **BOB**
8. the night before Christmas — **EVE**
9. pieces played alone — **SOLOS**
10. a musical engagement — **GIG**
11. another name for pop — **DAD**
12. radio device to locate objects — **RADAR**
13. Indy 500 vehicle (2 words) — **RACE CAR**
14. a good work done by a scout — **DEED**
15. a female sheep — **EWE**
16. tiny child — **TOT**
17. a joke played on someone — **GAG**
18. opposite of brother — **SIS**
19. Great! Super! — **WOW**
20. home of your iris and cornea — **EYE**

Challenge:
Cool palindrome sentences . . .
  Step on no pets!
Can you create more?

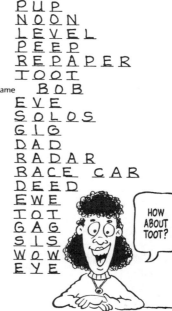

HOW ABOUT TOOT?

Too hot to hoot!

Page 47

Travel Time

Name _____

Summer Vacation

Summer vacation is almost here. It's time to plan a trip or two. Think about packing, means of transportation, and destinations as you complete this chart. Write words to fit each category using letters shown at the top of each column. Fill in as many words as you can in each box. You may use information sources to help your search. Then compare your answers to two or three classmates' answers, crossing out any words that are the same. Determine which person has the most items unmarked.

POSSIBILITIES INCLUDE

Category	T	R	I	P	S
Destinations	Tuscon Texas Tennessee Theme park	Resort Race Raleigh Racine Rally	Ireland Illinois Idaho Iceland Indy 500	Phoenix Pasadena Philadelphia Pittsburgh	Six Flags San Francisco
Items to pack	tent towels tennis shoes t-shirt	robe radio rod+reel ring	ice I.D. card intinerary Irish setter	popcorn pillow passport	suitcase sweat shirt sleeping bag
Means of travel	truck train	rail R.V. rowboat rental car	Isuzu	pick-up truck	Ship sail

LET'S GO!!

Page 48

Crack the Cheese Code

Name _____

June – Dairy Month

Count the holes in the pieces of cheese. Write that number beside the cheese. Then use the numbers to break the code. For example, if the number is $\overline{4}$, write the letter M. If the number is $\underline{4}$ write the letter J.

JUNE IS THE TIME
4 5 5 10   0 1   2 8 10   2 0 4 10

TO SALUTE AMERICAN
2 8   1 7 2 5 2 10   7 4 10 3 0 1 7 5

DAIRY PRODUCERS!
9 7 0 3 6   9 3 8 9 5 1 10 3 1

DID YOU KNOW THAT A
9 1 9   3 5 8   3 5 8 0 2 8 7 2   7

GOOD DAIRY COW MAY
6 8 8 9   9 7 0 3 6   1 8 0   4 7 6

WEIGH UP TO 1,700 POUNDS
0 10 0 6 8   8 9   2 8   9 8 8 5 9 1

AND PRODUCE 2,300 GALLONS
7 5 9   9 3 8 9 5 1 10   6 7 2 2 8 5 1

OR MORE OF MILK IN
8 3   4 8 3 10   8 10   4 0 2 3   0 5

A YEAR?
7   6 10 7 3

Page 49

Annual Tradition

Name _____

Donut Day

On June 1 and 2, Chicago holds Donut Days. This annual tradition recalls the donuts served to doughboys by the Salvation Army during WWI. Use the letters around the doughnuts to discover the names of other objects that have holes. Write the name of the object under each doughnut.

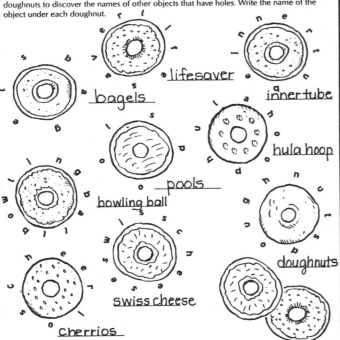

lifesaver
bagels
inner tube
hula hoop
pools
bowling ball
doughnuts
swiss cheese
cherrios

Page 50

Patchwork Pals

Name _____

End of School Year

Celebrate the year's end with a pal search. Ask classmates to autograph boxes that apply to them. A student may not sign more than two times. The event had to happen during this school year.

ANSWERS WILL VARY.

had a clean desk all year!	outgrew some clothes.	went on a field trip.	had a parent visit the class.
can name the 7 continents and 4 oceans.	ate somewhere new.	was in a play or recital.	played soccer.
wore red to school today.	went to a basketball game.	went on a weekend trip.	went to a concert.
helped the teacher.	new to our school this year.	made the class laugh.	went home from school sick.
got new shoes.	got braces on teeth.	got a haircut.	can correctly spell a word with 10 letters or more.
played on a school sports team.	got a new pet.	never missed a day of school.	moved to a new house or apartment.

Page 51

© Instructional Fair • TS Denison

IF8727 *Challenge Your Mind*

Happy Birthday U.S.

U.S. Independence Day

Name _____

Each year on the fourth of July, the United States celebrates its birthday and the adoption of the Declaration of Independence. Solve these rebus puzzles to uncover words and phrases associated with this holiday.

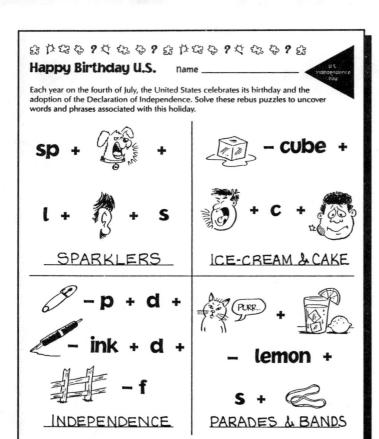

SPARKLERS

ICE-CREAM & CAKE

INDEPENDENCE

PARADES & BANDS

Page 52

Family Fun Times

U.S. Independence Day

Name _____

On the Fourth of July, families across the U.S. are getting together for fun and celebration. Find out what each family below is doing. Draw a line through the three words in a row that belong together. Write on the line the name of the activity or location from the Word Bank.

Word Bank

picnic	hiking
camping	beach
zoo	amusement park

Lee Family
CAMPING

drum	campfire	dog
dress	tent	backpack
bathing suit	sleeping bag	dessert

Ruiz Family
BEACH

water	sand	shells
fan	cat	TV
pillow	purse	shoes

Wallace Family
PICNIC

basket	swing	grass
table	roller coaster	games
food	monkeys	sister

Goldfarb Family
ZOO

flowers	pail	feeding time
rides	lions	roller coaster
cage	candy	music

Play tic-tac-toe with categories. Draw a large gameboard. Determine a category. Take turns writing words in the spaces. The first person to write three words in a row—across, down, or diagonally—is the winner.

Page 53

Twelve Months in a Year

Summer Vacation

Name _____

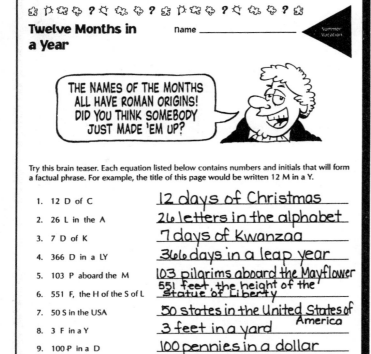

THE NAMES OF THE MONTHS ALL HAVE ROMAN ORIGINS! DID YOU THINK SOMEBODY JUST MADE 'EM UP?

Try this brain teaser. Each equation listed below contains numbers and initials that will form a factual phrase. For example, the title of this page would be written 12 M in a Y.

1. 12 D of C — 12 days of Christmas
2. 26 L in the A — 26 letters in the alphabet
3. 7 D of K — 7 days of Kwanzaa
4. 366 D in a LY — 366 days in a leap year
5. 103 P aboard the M — 103 pilgrims aboard the Mayflower
6. 551 F, the H of the S of L — 551 feet, the height of the Statue of Liberty
7. 50 S in the USA — 50 states in the United States of America
8. 3 F in a Y — 3 feet in a yard
9. 100 P in a D — 100 pennies in a dollar
10. 12 I in a F — 12 inches in a foot

Page 54

Have a Ball!

Summer Vacation

Name _____

There's nothing better than a game of baseball on a summer day. How well do you know your baseball terms? Count the strings on each baseball. Write the amount on each baseball. Then use the letters above and below the baseball to break the code.

1. $\overline{5}\,\overline{1}\,\overline{5}\,\overline{4}\;\overline{7}\,\overline{10}\;\overline{5}\,\overline{1}\,\overline{8}\,\overline{8}\;\overline{5}$ — BASE ON BALLS
2. $\overline{10}\,\overline{7}\,\overline{4}\,\overline{9}\;\overline{3}\,\overline{4}\,\overline{9}$ — PITCHER
3. $\overline{7}\,\overline{10}\,\overline{4}\;\overline{4}\,\overline{10}\;\overline{4}\,\overline{7}\,\overline{7}\,\overline{10}\,\overline{1}\,\overline{8}$ $\overline{3}\,\overline{1}\,\overline{8}\,\overline{2}$ — INTENTIONAL WALK
4. $\overline{3}\,\overline{7}\,\overline{6}\,\overline{4}\;\overline{10}\,\overline{8}\,\overline{1}\,\overline{4}\,\overline{4}$ — HOME PLATE
5. $\overline{4}\,\overline{10}\,\overline{4}\,\overline{9}\,\overline{7}\;\overline{7}\,\overline{10}\,\overline{10}\,\overline{7}\,\overline{10}\,\overline{1}\,\overline{5}$ — EXTRA INNINGS
6. $\overline{9}\,\overline{11}\,\overline{10}\,\overline{5}\;\overline{5}\,\overline{1}\,\overline{4}\,\overline{4}\,\overline{4}\,\overline{11}\;\;\overline{7}\,\overline{10}$ — RUNS BATTED IN
7. $\overline{5}\,\overline{4}\,\overline{9}\;\overline{7}\,\overline{2}\,\overline{4}\,\overline{7}\;\overline{11}\,\overline{4}$ — STRIKE OUT
8. $\overline{11}\,\overline{2}\,\overline{1}\,\overline{6}\;\overline{7}\,\overline{10}\,\overline{11}$ — DIAMOND
9. $\overline{11}\;\overline{11}\,\overline{1}\,\overline{7}\;\overline{11}\,\overline{4}$ — DUGOUT
10. $\overline{6}\,\overline{1}\,\overline{0}\,\overline{7}\,\overline{9}\;\overline{8}\,\overline{4}\,\overline{1}\,\overline{1}\,\overline{4}$ — MAJOR LEAGUE
11. $\overline{10}\;\overline{7}\,\overline{5}\,\overline{7}\,\overline{4}\,\overline{7}\;\overline{7}\,\overline{10}\,\overline{5}$ — POSITIONS
12. $\overline{7}\,\overline{11}\,\overline{4}\,\overline{2}\,\overline{2}\,\overline{4}\,\overline{8}\;\overline{11}\,\overline{4}\,\overline{9}$ — OUTFIELDER
13. $\overline{9}\,\overline{1}\,\overline{4}\,\overline{9}\,\overline{3}\,\overline{4}\,\overline{9}$ — CATCHER
14. $\overline{9}\,\overline{7}\,\overline{7}\,\overline{2}\,\overline{7}\,\overline{4}$ — ROOKIE
15. $\overline{3}\,\overline{7}\,\overline{9}\,\overline{8}\,\overline{11}\;\overline{5}\,\overline{4}\,\overline{9}\,\overline{7}\,\overline{4}\,\overline{5}$ — WORLD SERIES
16. $\overline{11}\;\overline{10}\,\overline{7}\,\overline{2}\,\overline{7}\,\overline{9}\,\overline{6}\,\overline{5}$ — UNIFORMS
17. $\overline{10}\;\overline{4}\,\overline{7}\,\overline{10}\;\overline{10}\,\overline{1}\,\overline{7}\,\overline{10}\,\overline{4}$ — PENNANT
18. $\overline{4}\,\overline{4}\,\overline{1}\,\overline{6}\,\overline{6}\;\overline{1}\,\overline{4}\,\overline{4}\,\overline{5}$ — TEAMMATES
19. $\overline{3}\,\overline{7}\,\overline{6}\,\overline{4}\;\;\overline{9}\,\overline{11}\,\overline{10}$ — HOME RUN

Page 55

IF8727 *Challenge Your Mind*

Rebus Riddle

Summer Vacation

Name _____

August is the perfect time for a picnic. Hot summer days and refreshing drinks go hand-in-hand. Read the rebus puzzles to discover a riddle and its answer.

Riddle: WHAT DO FROGS DRINK AT PICNICS?

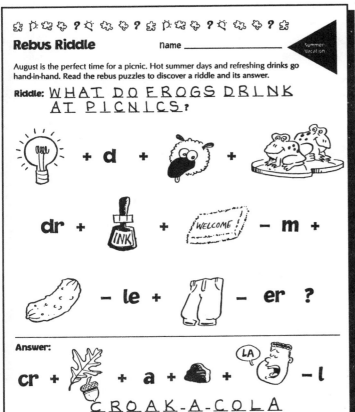

Answer:

cr + 🍂 + a + 🪨 + (LA) 😀 − l

C R O A K - A - C O L A

Page 56

Sun and Fun

Name _____

Career Ca...

In 1894, Pre... to be calle...

The second Sunday in August is Family Day and a perfect t... picnics. Add a straight line to each letter below to create a...

1. ANTS
2. VOLLEYBALL
3. BEACH
4. SUNSHINE
5. FISHING
6. BLANKET
7. SWIMMING
8. SANDWICHES

AUGUST IS NAMED AFTER AUGUSTUS, THE FIRST ROMAN EMPEROR! PASS THE MUSTARD!

Page 57

"According to Hoyle"

Name _____

Hoyle Day

On August 29 we remember Edmond Hoyle. He lived in London during the early 1700s, and for many years gave instructions in the playing of games. Celebrate the day by solving this wordsearch about fun and games.

```
C R A Z Y E I G H T S O C C E R C E B
O N R M I N I G O L F S H P X O O C O
M I C H E C K E R S S O L A L M E A
P W H O C K E Y J E R L T L L P I R
U T E A M S L K H T P A S F R E E P D
T R R S V O C O M B G U B G R T V G
E I Y E Q U M G U T K N T A N B I I A
R V L L L T X E F M I R S I L T M D
G I L U L B I K I N G C C K M A I E E
A A A R E C S P O R T A O T M D O O S
M T R S Y A C W A T E R S K I I N G N
E S E L B R A M Y T E F A S W N J A N
S E L L A B E S A B L L I K S N G C M N
C H A L L E N G E T I C T A C T O E F
O F X O L I D I C E R I A T L O S T
```

Word Box

chess	soccer	relax	videogames	roller blading	competition
teams	baseball	fun	jumprope	swimming	computer
dice	volleyball	win	crazy eights	racing	games
luck	basketball	piece	go fish	tic-tac-toe	trivia
rules	biking	archery	mini golf	solitaire	marbles
sport	waterskiing	checkers	tennis	net	hockey
safety	challenge	skill	rally	board games	

Page 58

Summer Scramble

Name _____

Summer Vacation

There's nothing like a little word play on a hot summer day. See how many words you can make from the letters in the scrambled word. Then use all the scrambled letters to make a word that tells who would rather work with numbers than words. Write your answer above the score box. POSSIBILITIES INCLUDE

I n T M A C I T S E A H A M

2-letter words

am	hi
at	it
is	as
he	ma
in	ah
me	I'm
an	sí

3-letter words

men	ant
ate	sat
has	ham
met	his
hit	can
cat	ice
met	tie

4-letter words

cast	mice
stem	sent
meat	main
mate	east
time	this
math	cash
team	that

5-letter words

chime	shame
steam	meant
teach	mimic
state	teams
match	mania
stain	saint
share	hints

6 or more-letter words

stitch	machines
mitten	chemist
attach	imitate
insect	cinema
chants	mathematics

Answer: mathematicians

SCORE	
S	0–10 words—Just playing around
C	11–15 words—Still pretty cool
O	16–20 words—Getting warm
R	21–30 words—Turn on the fan!
E	31 or more—Hot stuff!

Page 59

Page 60

...pers   Name _____

...dent Cleveland signed a bill declaring the first Monday in November
...d Labor Day in honor of American workers.

GROVER CLEVELAND IS THE ONLY U.S. PRESIDENT TO SERVE TWO NON-CONSECUTIVE TERMS OF OFFICE!

Unscramble the letters below to identify each description given. Which work sounds most interesting to you? _____

Description	Scrambled Letters	Job
1. makes, finishes, and repairs wooden structures	p n r t e a r c e	CARPENTER
2. designs structures, machines, and systems	n i e n e g r e	ENGINEER
3. provides medical treatment	o t r c d o	DOCTOR
4. repairs machines, vehicles, or tools	i n a c m e h c	MECHANIC
5. transmits messages over the air	r o b d c t r s a e a	BROADCASTER
6. studies forms of life from prehistoric times	o t o l a e n i g o t l p s	PALEONTOLOGIST
7. hears and decides cases in a court of law	e g u j d	JUDGE
8. creates with words	h o t u a r	AUTHOR
9. keeps and checks financial records	t a o u c n c n t a	ACCOUNTANT
10. provides medical care to animals	n r a n r e t v e i a i	VETERINARIAN

Page 60

Page 61

September... Remember?

Name _____

It's September. Time to sharpen your memory skills. Fold back the bottom half of this paper. Then study the picture for 3–5 minutes. Flip your paper and answer the questions. Open to the picture to see how you did.

1. What time is it? 9:00 What is the room number? 201
2. How many student desks? None.
3. What is the weather like? sunny, some clouds
4. What is on the file cabinet? A plant
5. Who is the teacher? Mrs. Sandy
6. What is under the windows? A bookcase
7. What math problem is on the chalkboard? 6 x 8 = 48
8. How many windows are in the door? 2
9. How many chalkboard erasers? 3
10. How many drawers are in the file cabinet? 3
11. What is between the windows and the chalkboard? A computer
12. What word is above the windows? TEAMWORK
13. Where is the flag? Next to the clock
14. What is in the southwest corner? An aquarium

Page 61

Page 62

Hidden, No "Kidden"

Name _____

The words in the schoolhouse are hidden in these sentences. They may be found in the middle of a word or by combining the end of one word with the beginning of the next. Highlight each word found. The first one is done for you.

1. Would you like more tea, Cheryl?
2. "Open cilantro for flavoring," suggested the chef.
3. Mark, erase the boards, please.
4. Skid slowly on soft ice.
5. Your program does not compute, Rachael.
6. Nab oysters from the shells on Nantucket Island.
7. "Move the llama, then the zebra," ordered the director of the San Diego Zoo.
8. Clap, please, after the dance recital.
9. Ziggy, my favorite cartoon character, is bald.
10. When is the Valentine's Day party?
11. The Olympian figure skater made skating look easy.
12. The label looked like that in a J.C. Penney shirt.
13. Was Allegra destroyed by criticism?
14. Pa, in tse-tse flies, are there stingers that cause sleeping sickness?
15. My pa, personally, is the best dad in the world.
16. My instructor always reminds me to think before I act.
17. The past encourages the future.
18. The orchestra includes a viola, bass, and violins.

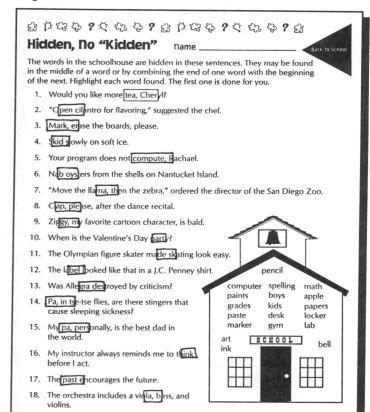

pencil
computer spelling math
paints boys apple
grades kids papers
paste desk locker
marker gym lab
art SCHOOL bell
ink

Page 62

Page 63

Patriotic Papers

Name _____

On September 8 and September 17, Americans honor the two documents important to the country's history. Discover some facts about these patriotic papers by supplying the vowels which time and aging have eroded.

1. Sptmbr 8 s Ntnl Pldg f llgnc Dy. September 8 is National Pledge of Allegiance Day.
2. Kds frst rctd th pldg s thy sltd th flg n 1892. Kids first recited the pledge as they saluted the flag in 1892.
3. n 1954, th wrds "ndr Gd" wr ddd. In 1954, the words "Under God" were added.
4. Sptmbr 17 s th nnvrsry f th sgnng f th Cnstttn f th ntd stts. September 17 is the anniversary of the signing of the Constitution of the United States.
5. Ths dcmnt sts frth th lws f th cntry nd th rgts f th ppl. This document sets forth the laws of the country and the rights of the people.
6. Th sgnng tk plc t ndpndnc Hll n Phldlph, Pnnslvn, n 1787. The signing took place at Independence Hall in Philadelphia, Pennsylvania.
7. Jms Mdsn ws clld th "Fthr f th Cnstttn," bt Gvrnr Mrrs ctly wrt t. James Madison was called the "Father of the Constitution" but Governor Morris actually wrote it.
8. Th rgnl Cnstttn s dsplyd n th Ntnl rchvs Bldng n Wshngtn, D.C. The original Constitution is displayed in the National Archives Building in Washington, D.C.

Page 63

© Instructional Fair • TS Denison

IF8727 *Challenge Your Mind*

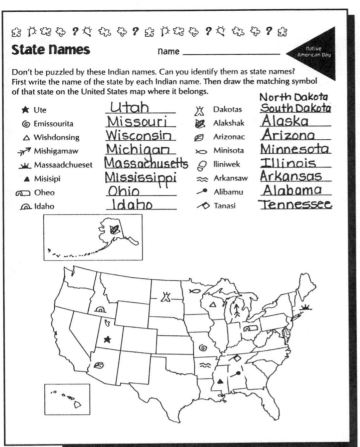

State Names

Name _____

Native American Day

Don't be puzzled by these Indian names. Can you identify them as state names? First write the name of the state by each Indian name. Then draw the matching symbol of that state on the United States map where it belongs.

★ Ute — Utah
◎ Emissourita — Missouri
△ Wishdonsing — Wisconsin
✈ Mishigamaw — Michigan
🔱 Massaadchueset — Massachusetts
▲ Misisipi — Mississippi
⌂ Oheo — Ohio
⌂ Idaho — Idaho

✗ Dakotas — North Dakota / South Dakota
🦋 Alakshak — Alaska
✿ Arizonac — Arizona
🍃 Minisota — Minnesota
🐚 Iliniwek — Illinois
〰 Arkansaw — Arkansas
✒ Alibamu — Alabama
◇ Tanasi — Tennessee

Football Fame Frames

Name _____

Fall Sport

It's a forward pass (horizontal, vertical, or diagonal) into the Wordsearch Hall of Fame. Block the football words found on the locker room wall.

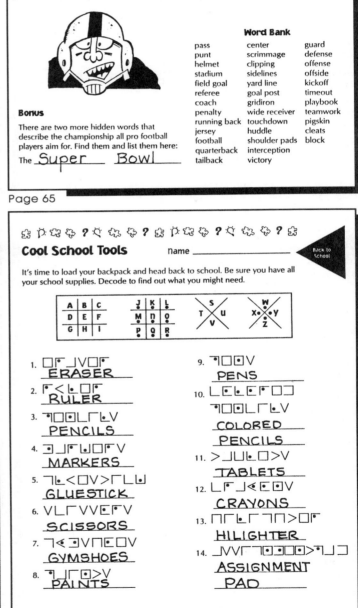

Word Bank

pass	center	guard
punt	scrimmage	defense
helmet	clipping	offense
stadium	sidelines	offside
field goal	yard line	kickoff
referee	goal post	timeout
coach	gridiron	playbook
penalty	wide receiver	teamwork
running back	touchdown	pigskin
jersey	huddle	cleats
football	shoulder pads	block
quarterback	interception	
tailback	victory	

Bonus

There are two more hidden words that describe the championship all pro football players aim for. Find them and list them here:

The _Super_ _Bowl_

Sing a Song of Apples

Name _____

Johnny Appleseed's Birthday

John Chapman, born on September 26, 1774, was better known as Johnny Appleseed. Number the apple words in alphabetical order. Then write the words in the matching blanks to finish this song to honor Johnny. (Tune: Bicycle Built for Two.)

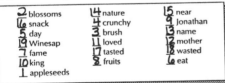

3 blossoms	14 nature	15 near
16 snack	4 crunchy	9 Jonathan
5 day	3 brush	13 name
19 Winesap	11 loved	12 mother
7 fame	17 tasted	18 wasted
10 king	8 fruits	6 eat
1 appleseeds		

Johnny, Johnny Appleseed was his _name_,
Planting _appleseeds_ awarded him much _fame_,
The appleseeds once were _wasted_,
'Til Johnny's apples were _tasted_.
Then far and _near_, through the land he "_loved_" so dear,
Apple _blossoms_ were everywhere.

Apples, apples, the _king_ of _fruits_ they say,
Apples, apples, _eat_ one every _day_,
They're _mother_ _nature_ 's toothbrush,
So eat one if you can't _brush_,
A _Jonathan_, _Winesap_ or McIntosh,
They're a _crunchy_ _snack_, by gosh!

Cool School Tools

Name _____

Back to School

It's time to load your backpack and head back to school. Be sure you have all your school supplies. Decode to find out what you might need.

A B C	J K L		S	W
D E F	M N O		T U V	X Y Z
G H I	P Q R			

1. ERASER
2. RULER
3. PENCILS
4. MARKERS
5. GLUESTICK
6. SCISSORS
7. GYMSHOES
8. PAINTS
9. PENS
10. COLORED PENCILS
11. TABLETS
12. CRAYONS
13. HILIGHTER
14. ASSIGNMENT PAD

IF8727 *Challenge Your Mind*

Page 68

8 Is Great!

Name _____

October

The origin of the word October is from the Latin word *Octobris*, which means eight. Many other words begin with the prefix "Oct". Use each definition to help you unscramble the words.

Meaning

1. goatnoc — OCTAGON — 8-sided polygon
2. toect — OCTET — 8 lines of poetry
3. stopocu — OCTOPUS — carnivorous 8-tentacled mollusk
4. vetoca — OCTAVE — 8 degrees between 2 musical tones
5. coodpot — OCTOPOD — 8-tentacled mollusk
6. togarneocnai — OCTOGENARIAN — a person between 80 and 90 years old
7. coheatnord — OCTAHEDRON — 8-surfaced polyhedron
8. cotteamer — OCTAMETER — verse with 8 metrical feet

Write the letters of the word *octameter* in the figure 8.

```
R      O
 E    C
   T
 A    E
   M
```

Page 68

Page 69

Greetings Neighbor!

Name _____

National Good Neighbor Month

On September 23, National Good Neighbor Day, take time to appreciate your neighbors. Discover some words about neighbors and neighborhoods by filling in the blanks with words that explain the clues. The word in the vertical box is the essence of good neighborhoods.

1. S A F E T Y
2. R E S P E C T
3. C O M M U N I T Y
4. C A R E
5. N E X T   D O O R
6. C H I L D R E N
7. S H A R E
8. H E L P
9. C L O S E - K N I T
10. B L O C K P A R T Y

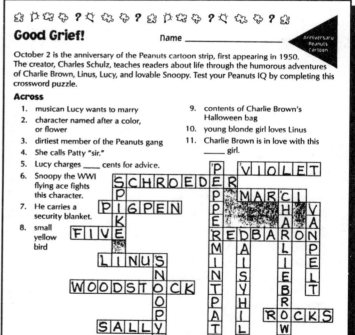

HOWDY!!

1. community watch programs promote _____
2. to show consideration
3. a group with common interests
4. concern for others
5. adjacent houses are _____ _____ to each other
6. youngest members of a neighborhood
7. to loan a possession is to _____
9. socially interwoven
10. celebration involving a street full of people

Page 69

Page 70

Good Times!

Name _____

October — National Clock Month

October is National Clock Month, so let the good "times" roll! Decode these timely words by writing the letters from the clocks above the hours. Underlined hours come from Clock II. Then match the definitions by placing the letters of the definitions before the decoded words. The first one has been done for you.

Clock I
```
    L  A  B
  K         C
  J         D
  I         E
    H  G  F
```

Clock II
```
    Z  M  N
  X         O
  W         P
  V         R
    U  T  S
```

D 1. time KEEPER
C 2. time BOMB (10-4-4-3-4-4)
J 3. time CAPSULE (1-2-12-1)
H 4. time LAPSE (2-12-3-5-2-7-11-4)
F 5. time SAVING (11-12-3-5-4)
L 6. time TABLE (5-12-8-1-6)
A 7. time WARP (6-12-1-11-4)
M 8. time ZONE (9-12-4-3)
E 9. time SHARE (11-2-1-4)
I 10. time MACHINE (5-7-12-4-4)
B 11. time CLOCK (12-12-2-7-8-1-4)
G 12. time EXPOSURE (2-11-12-2-11-4)
K 13. time FRAME (4-10-3-2-5-Z-4-4) (5-4-12-12-4)

A. a suspension of time
B. machine that stamps time cards
C. explosive
D. one who records time
E. joint ownership of vacation condo
F. expedient
G. photography term
H. camera technique
I. travel into the past or future
J. artifacts saved for the future
K. given period of time
L. transportation schedule
M. geographical region of like standard times

Page 70

Page 71

Good Grief!

Name _____

Anniversary Peanuts Cartoon

October 2 is the anniversary of the Peanuts cartoon strip, first appearing in 1950. The creator, Charles Schulz, teaches readers about life through the humorous adventures of Charlie Brown, Linus, Lucy, and lovable Snoopy. Test your Peanuts IQ by completing this crossword puzzle.

Across

1. musican Lucy wants to marry
2. character named after a color, or flower
3. dirtiest member of the Peanuts gang
4. She calls Patty "sir."
5. Lucy charges _____ cents for advice.
6. Snoopy the WWI flying ace fights this character.
7. He carries a security blanket.
8. small yellow bird
9. contents of Charlie Brown's Halloween bag
10. young blonde girl loves Linus
11. Charlie Brown is in love with this _____ girl.

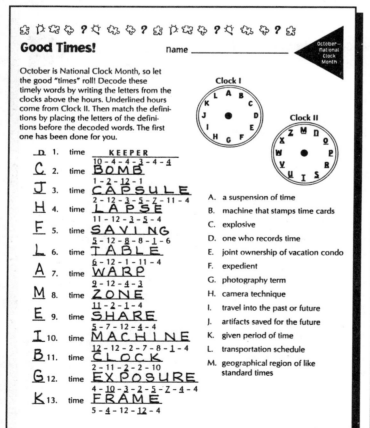

Down

1. Snoopy's desert-dwelling brother
2. Freckled; wears sandals
3. Snoopy was born at _____ _____ Puppy Farm.
4. baseball team's pitcher
5. Lucy's last name
6. Who is Joe Cool?

Page 71

© Instructional Fair • TS Denison

IF8727 *Challenge Your Mind*

120

National Pastime

Name _____

Baseball Season

The first radio broadcast of a World Series baseball game occurred on October 5, 1921. Print the names of the given baseball teams in ABC order on the lines below. Then write the letters in the circles on the lines at the bottom of the page to decode the message.

1. Ⓐ S T R O S
2. B R Ⓐ V E S
3. C Ⓐ R D I N A L S
4. C Ⓤ B S
5. D Ⓞ D G E R S
6. Ⓔ X P O S
7. Ⓖ I A N T S
8. M A R Ⓛ I N S
9. M E T S
10. P Ⓐ D R E S
11. P H I Ⓛ L I E S
12. P I R Ⓐ T E S
13. R Ⓔ D S
14. R O C K Ⓘ E S

THE WORLD SERIES BEGAN IN 1903!

Teams
- Marlins
- Padres
- Phillies
- Giants
- Rockies
- Cardinals
- Reds
- Dodgers
- Braves
- Mets
- Astros
- Expos
- Pirates
- Cubs

These teams belong to the:

N A T I O N A L   L E A G U E
8² 10 12 14 5 3 1 8¹   11 13 2 7 4 6

* 8¹ = 1st circled letter   8² = 2nd circled letter

Page 72

Learn Not to Burn

Name _____

Fire Prevention Week October

Fire Prevention Week is observed the second week in October. Write the letters backward in order to name the most common causes of needless fires.

1. gniyalp htiw sehctam — playing with matches
2. dedaolrevo lacirtcele steltuo — overloaded electrical outlets
3. gnikoms ni deb — smoking in bed
4. gnirots elbammalf sdiuqil raen a ecanruf — storing flammable liquids near a furnace
5. gnisu enilosag ot trats eht llirg — using gasoline to start the grill
6. gnikooc stnedicca — cooking accidents
7. gniworht yawa gninrub setteragic — throwing away burning cigarettes
8. gnirots ylio, ysaerg ro tniap sgar — storing oily, greasy, or paint rags
9. ecaps sretaeh oot esolc ot scirbaf — space heaters too close to fabrics
10. kcabhsalf serif morf elbammalf diuqil semuf — flashback fires from flammable liquid fumes

FIRE SAFETY IS NO ACCIDENT!

Page 73

Hail, Columbus!

Name _____

Columbus Day

October 12, 1492 Christopher Columbus first sighted land. In honor of this event, Columbus Day became a national holiday in 1971. It is celebrated on the second Monday in October. Unscramble the words and write them in the correct blanks to learn more about Columbus.

Columbus was not trying to prove the world was **round** as many believe.
(dprun)
Instead, he wanted to find a shorter **route** to the **Indies** to build
(teuro)   (lsiend)
greater **trade** between the East and the West. After **seven** years of
(daret)   (venes)
trying, Columbus finally **convinced** **King** Ferdinand and Queen Isabella
(dincoevnc)   (gnik)
of Spain to **finance** his voyage. They gave him three ships, the **Nina**,
(nanefic)   (anin)
the **Pinta** and the **Santa** **Maria**. They also provided 90
(paint)   (antsa) (ramia)
crewmembers, supplies and made him an **admiral**. He could govern any lands he
(lamidra)
discovered and could have a share in **treasures** found and **future**
(ridvocsdee)   (utesarers)   (turfeu)
trading. He set sail on August 3, 1492 and land was sighted October 12, 1492. He landed
on an **island** he named San Salvador and called the people there
(daslni)
Indians, mistakenly thinking he had landed in the Indies, near Japan. He made
(sandini)
three more **voyages** to the New World, opening it to **Europeans**.
(yagvoe)   (upornease)

COLUMBUS, OHIO WAS THE FIRST U.S. CITY PLANNED & BUILT AS A STATE CAPITAL!

Page 74

Aardvark to Zebra

Name _____

Noah Webster's Birthday - Oct. 6

Noah Webster must have enjoyed words immensely to have written the first American dictionary. Use the clues below to determine the double-letter alphabet words. Write each word in the space provided.

AA - **AARDVARK** African mammal
BB - **RABBIT** synonym for hare or bunny
CC - **RACCOON** masked animal with ringed tail
DD - **HIDDEN** not in sight
EE - **WILDEBEEST** fastest land animal
FF - **STUFFING** bread cooked inside a turkey
GG - **EGG** where a yellow yolk is found
HH - **HITCHHIKE** to thumb a ride
II - **SKIING** sliding down a snowy slope
LL - **SHELL** the home of a hermit crab
MM - **HAMMER** a pounding tool
NN - **FUNNY** humorous
OO - **COOKIE** a chocolate-chip treat
PP - **HIPPO** large water mammal
RR - **SORRY** feeling bad about something you did
SS - **CROSSWORD** across and down clue-type puzzle
TT - **SHUTTLE** a spacecraft that lands like an airplane
UU - **VACUUM** a sweeper
ZZ - **DRIZZLE** light rain

NOAH WEBSTER WAS ALSO A FOUNDER OF AMHERST COLLEGE!

Page 75

Lady Liberty

Name _____

The Statue of Liberty was dedicated on October 28, 1886. Celebrate Lady Liberty's birthday by using the coordinate code to discover the facts about this national treasure.

C	R	O	W	N
	J	L	H	
M	W	Y	P	F
T	E	A	R	U
C	X	O	I	B
S	G	Z	V	N
	Q	D	K	

IT WAS COMPLETED IN PARIS IN 1884! SACRÉ BLEU!

1. The statue's real name is "Liberty" R-3, N-5, O-1, W-4, R-5, W-1, C-3, R-3, N-5, W-4, N-5, R-5 __ENLIGHTENING__ the World."

2. It is made of C-4, O-4, W-2, W-2, R-3, W-3 ___COPPER___ .

3. It was a gift of N-2, W-3, W-4, R-3, N-5, O-6, C-5, W-1, W-4, W-2 ___FRIENDSHIP___ from France.

4. The U.S.A. raised $280,000 for the W-2, R-3, O-6, R-3, C-5, C-3, O-3, O-1 ___PEDESTAL___ on which to place the statue.

5. Her crown has a 25-window O-4, N-4, C-5, R-3, W-3, W-5, O-3, C-3, W-4, O-4, N-5 __OBSERVATION__ platform.

6. An R-3, O-1, R-3, W-5, O-3, C-3, O-4, W-3 ___ELEVATOR___ carries visitors from the pedestal to the foot of the statue.

7. Spiral C-5, C-3, O-3, W-4, W-3, R-2, O-3, O-2, C-5 __STAIRWAYS__ move people from the base to the crown.

8. R-3, C-2, C-2, O-3 O-1, O-3, O-5, O-3, W-3, N-3, C-5 ___EMMA___ __LAZARUS__ wrote a poem inscribed on the pedestal in 1903.

9. The poem's most famous line begins R-5, W-4, W-5, R-3 C-2, R-3 O-2, O-4, N-3, W-3 C-3, W-4, W-3, R-3, O-6 O-2, O-4, N-3, W-3 W-2, O-4, O-4, W-3 __GIVE__ __ME__ __YOUR__ __TIRED__, __YOUR__ __POOR__ .

Hiddles (Halloween Riddles)

Name _____

Hey diddle, hiddle, try these Halloween riddles. To answer the riddles, write the letter that comes alphabetically before each letter listed.

1. What was the all-ghost baseball team called?
   VIF CPP KBZT __The Boo Jays__

2. What is a ghost's favorite dance?
   VIF CVH-B-CPP __The Bug-a-boo__

3. What's green, lies on hamburgers, and has fangs?
   B WBNQJDLMF __A vampickle__

4. Why was the Egyptian Kid homesick?
   IF NJTTFE IJT NVNNZ __He missed his mummy.__

5. How did Sammy Spine open his door?
   With a . . . TLFMFUPO LFZ __skeleton key__

6. What do you call Casper's long-distance calls?
   HIPTV UP HIPTV __ghost to ghost__

7. What does a police vampire say?
   GBOH ZPV __fang you__

8. What do you call a ghost who broke his leg?
   B IPCCMJO' HPCMJO __A hobblin' goblin__

9. What is the worst occupation in the world?
   ESBDVMB'T EFOUJTU __Dracula's dentist__

10. Why was papa ghost uncomfortable?
    Someone put . . . TUBSDI JO IJT TIFFU __Starch in his sheet__

11. What is a ghost's favorite attraction at amusement parks?
    VIF SPMMFS HIPTUFS __The roller ghoster__

MY FAVORITE DESSERT IS BOO-BERRY PIE!

Page 76 / Page 77

Spooky Wordsearch

Name _____

Circle the spooky words in orange and black. (↑, →, ↓, ←, ↙, ↗, ↖, ↘)

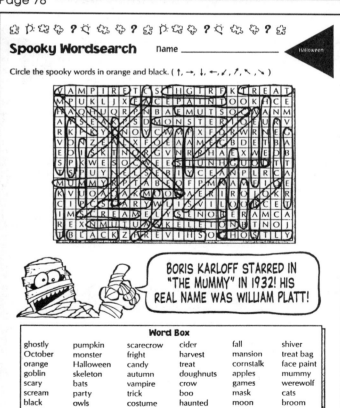

BORIS KARLOFF STARRED IN "THE MUMMY" IN 1932! HIS REAL NAME WAS WILLIAM PLATT!

Word Box

ghostly	pumpkin	scarecrow	cider	fall	shiver
October	monster	fright	harvest	mansion	treat bag
orange	Halloween	candy	treat	cornstalk	face paint
goblin	skeleton	autumn	doughnuts	apples	mummy
scary	bats	vampire	crow	games	werewolf
scream	party	trick	boo	mask	cats
black	owls	costume	haunted	moon	broom
spooky					bones

Hallo–sing!

Name _____

Create a crazy song! Fold this page on the dotted line. While the right side is out of sight, write words in the blanks on the left. Then unfold the page and place your word choices in the song. Sing it to a friend! ANSWERS WILL VARY.

1. _____ relative
2. _____ noun beginning with a vowel
3. _____ plural noun
4. _____ plural noun
5. _____ plural noun
6. _____ plural noun
7. _____ plural noun
8. _____ plural noun
9. _____ plural noun
10. _____ plural noun
11. _____ plural noun
12. _____ plural noun
13. _____ plural noun

On the first day of Halloween, my ___1___ gave to me an ___2___ in a dead tree.
On the second day of Halloween, my ___1___ gave to me ___3___ and a ___2___ in a dead tree.
On the third day of Halloween, my ___1___ gave to me ___4___ and an ___2___ in a dead tree.
On the fourth day of Halloween, my ___1___ gave to me ___5___ and an ___2___ in a dead tree.
On the fifth day of Halloween, my ___1___ gave to me ___6___ and an ___2___ in a dead tree.
On the sixth day of Halloween, my ___1___ gave to me ___7___ and an ___2___ in a dead tree.
On the seventh day of Halloween, my ___1___ gave to me ___8___ and an ___2___ in a dead tree.
On the eighth day of Halloween, my ___1___ gave to me ___9___ and an ___2___ in a dead tree.
On the ninth day of Halloween, my ___1___ gave to me ___10___ and an ___2___ in a dead tree.
On the tenth day of Halloween, my ___1___ gave to me ___11___ and an ___2___ in a dead tree.
On the eleventh day of Halloween, my ___1___ gave to me ___12___ and an ___2___ in a dead tree.
On the twelfth day of Halloween, my ___1___ gave to me ___13___ and an ___2___ in a dead tree.

Page 78 / Page 79

A Halloween BOO-st!   Name _____

Halloween

Give your October a boo-st by learning the language of the ghosts. Each word contains the letters—*boo*.

boom	booboo	boomerang
boogie	booster shot	boot
booth	booster seat	

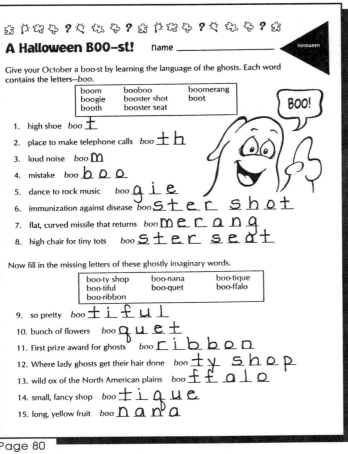

BOO!

1. high shoe   boo **t**
2. place to make telephone calls   boo **th**
3. loud noise   boo **m**
4. mistake   boo **boo**
5. dance to rock music   boo **gie**
6. immunization against disease   boo **ster shot**
7. flat, curved missile that returns   boo **merang**
8. high chair for tiny tots   boo **ster seat**

Now fill in the missing letters of these ghostly imaginary words.

boo-ty shop	boo-nana	boo-tique
boo-tiful	boo-quet	boo-ffalo
boo-ribbon		

9. so pretty   boo **tiful**
10. bunch of flowers   boo **quet**
11. First prize award for ghosts   boo **ribbon**
12. Where lady ghosts get their hair done   boo **ty shop**
13. wild ox of the North American plains   boo **ffalo**
14. small, fancy shop   boo **tique**
15. long, yellow fruit   boo **nana**

Page 80

Spooky Speakers   Name _____

Halloween

Decipher the message of each Haunted Halloweener. Unscramble the word order and write the sentences on the lines.

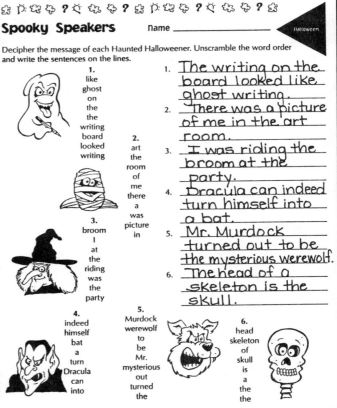

1. like ghost on the the writing board looked writing

2. art the room of me there a was picture in

3. broom I at the riding was the party

4. indeed himself bat a turn Dracula can into

5. Murdock werewolf to be Mr. mysterious out turned the

6. head skeleton of skull is a the the

1. The writing on the board looked like ghost writing.
2. There was a picture of me in the art room.
3. I was riding the broom at the party.
4. Dracula can indeed turn himself into a bat.
5. Mr. Murdock turned out to be the mysterious werewolf.
6. The head of a skeleton is the skull.

Page 81

Four Heads Are Better Than One   Name _____

Mount Rushmore Completed

Mount Rushmore National Memorial was finished on October 31, 1941. Decode the words. Place the corresponding letters of the words in the blanks below to match facts about this famous monument.

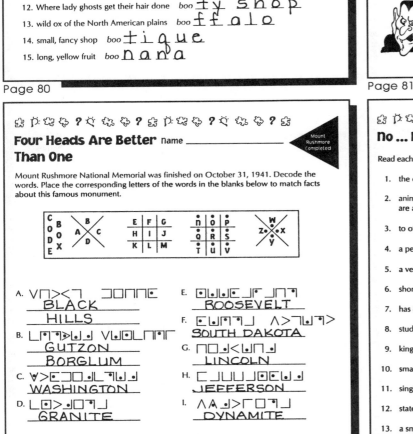

CODE BOX

A. **BLACK HILLS**
B. **GUTZON BORGLUM**
C. **WASHINGTON**
D. **GRANITE**
E. **ROOSEVELT**
F. **SOUTH DAKOTA**
G. **LINCOLN**
H. **JEFFERSON**
I. **DYNAMITE**

C 1. America's first president
H 2. Second head on the mount
D 3. Substance from which the heads are carved
I 4. "Tool" used to carve the likenesses
B 5. Man who designed the memorial
G 6. 16th American president
A 7. The mount is part of this range
F 8. State that houses this memorial
E 9. President between Jefferson and Lincoln

Page 82

No ... No ... November   Name _____

November

Read each clue. Write an answer that contains the letters *no*. Get ready, get set . . . No!

1. the eleventh month   **November**
2. animals that sleep during the day and are active at night   **nocturnal**
3. to offer as an election candidate   **nominate**
4. a person, place, or thing   **noun**
5. a vehicle for snow travel   **snowmobile**
6. short tube on the end of a hose   **nozzle**
7. has 88 black and white keys   **piano**
8. study of the ocean   **oceanography**
9. king of the dinosaurs   **tyrannosaurus**
10. small fish often used for bait   **minnow**
11. single-railed track   **monorail**
12. state on the east coast of the U.S.   **North Carolina**
13. a small round hill   **knoll**
14. 12:00 P.M.   **noon**
15. average, ordinary   **normal**
16. star named Polaris   **North Star**
17. a Scandinavian country   **Norway**

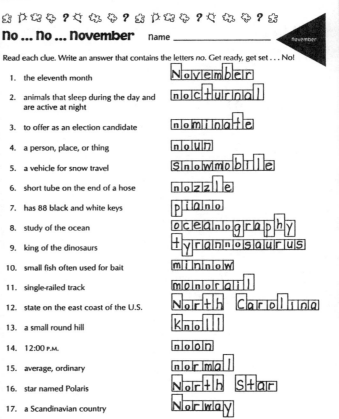

Page 83

IF8727 *Challenge Your Mind*

I'll Have a "Montagu" with Pickle

Name _____

John Montagu, the Fourth Earl of Sandwich, was born on November 3. When this English nobleman was playing cards, he did not want to stop to eat his meal. He had a servant place meat and cheese between two slices of bread so he could eat with one hand and play cards with the other. He is credited with inventing the "sandwich." Unscramble the names of these "inventors" to see which kind of sandwich they invented. The first one is done for you.

1. Marie Buns ___submarine___
2. G.M.I. Bac ___Big Mac___
3. Toree B. Saf ___roast beef___
4. Shadee E. Manch ___ham and cheese___
5. Doeny Cog ___coney dog___
6. Shirlee G. Cleed ___grilled cheese___
7. F. His ___fish___
8. Chip F. Nerd ___french dip___
9. Path I. Kylles ___philly steak___
10. Lana A. Dust ___tuna salad___
11. Ken C. Hic ___chicken___
12. Barbee Cubfee ___beef barbecue___

JOHN MONTAGU HAD A LONG CAREER IN BRITISH POLITICS! YOU WANT FRIES WITH THAT?

Page 84

Hoops Hero

Name _____

Born on November 6, 1861, James Naismith was a gym teacher at a Massachusetts YMCA Training School. He wanted to develop an indoor winter game. So in 1891, using a soccer ball and two peach baskets, he invented the game we now refer to as basketball. Match these NBA teams with their city, state, or region.

E	1. Supersonics	A. Boston
K	2. Jazz	B. Los Angeles
I	3. Nuggets	C. Dallas
P	4. Bulls	D. Portland
B	5. Lakers	E. Seattle
N	6. 76ers	F. Houston
H	7. Hawks	G. Milwaukee
G	8. Bucks	H. Atlanta
O	9. Heat	I. Denver
F	10. Rockets	J. Phoenix
J	11. Suns	K. Utah
L	12. Knickerbockers	L. New York
C	13. Mavericks	M. Detroit
M	14. Pistons	N. Philadelphia
A	15. Celtics	O. Miami
D	16. Trail Blazers	P. Chicago
R	17. Hornets	Q. Orlando
Q	18. Magic	R. Charlotte

HE WAS BORN IN ALMONTE, ONTARIO, CANADA!

Page 85

Cele-BEAR-ties

Name _____

The first Sunday in November is Hug-a-Bear Sunday. Make it a Novem-BEAR to remem-BEAR! Identify these "famous" cele-BEAR-ties using the Code Den coordinates.

Code Den

	B	E	A	R
7	K	F	B	H
6	C	N	P	Q
5	S	V	X	X
4	J	U	G	D
3	Z	L	I	M
2	R	W	T	Y
1	A	E	I	O

1. a female aviator B-1, R-3, E-1, E-3, A-1, B-1 BEAR R-7, B-1, B-2, A-2
2. 16th U.S. president B-1, BEAR R-7, B-1, R-3 E-3, A-1, E-6, B-6, R-1, E-3, E-6
3. family of book heros BEAR E-1, E-6, B-5, A-2, B-1, A-1, E-6 BEAR B-5
4. American Patriot BEAR B-4, B-1, R-3, A-1, E-6 E-7, B-2, B-1, E-6, B-7, E-3, A-1, E-6
5. WWII flying ace A-2, R-7, E-1 B-2, E-1, R-4 BEAR R-1, E-6
6. African-American comedian A-7, A-1, E-3, E-3 B-6, R-1, B-5 BEAR
7. rock-and-roll king E-1, E-3, E-5, A-1, B-5 BEAR B-5, E-3, E-1, R-2

8. Tom Sawyer's pal R-7, E-4, B-6, B-7, E-3, E-1 BEAR R-2, E-7, A-1, E-6, E-6
9. children's author BEAR E-5, E-1, B-2, E-3, R-2 B-6, E-3, E-1, B-1, B-2, R-2
10. U.S. president A-2, E-1, R-4, R-4, R-2 BEAR B-2, R-1, R-1, B-5, E-1, E-5, E-1, E-3, A-2
11. scientific genius B-1, E-3 BEAR A-2 E-1, A-1, E-6, B-5, A-2, E-1, A-1, E-6
12. Red Cross founder B-6, E-3, B-1, B-2, B-1 BEAR A-2, R-1, E-6

1. Amelia BEAR-hart
2. A-BEAR-ham Lincoln
3. BEAR-enstain Bears
4. BEAR-jamin Franklin
5. The Red BEAR-on
6. Bill Cos-BEAR

7. Elvis BEAR-sley
8. Huckle-BEAR-y Finn
9. BEAR-verly Cleary
10. Teddy BEAR Roosevelt
11. Al-BEAR-t Einstein
12. Clara BEAR-ton

Page 86

I'm All Ears ...

Name _____

Steamboat Willie, a Walt Disney film, was the first animated talking cartoon. Mickey Mouse debuted in this film on November 18, 1928. Count the holes in Mickey's cheese blocks. Write that number beside the cheese. Then use the letters above and below the cheese to break the code. Example: $\overline{4}$ = M and $\underline{4}$ = B. How many of these Disney movies have you viewed?

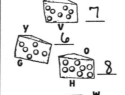

1. $2\,0\overline{8}5\ \ 3\,0\underline{5}6$ LION KING
2. $9\,0\underline{5}\overline{8}11\overline{8}0\overline{8}$ PINOCCHIO
3. $4\overline{7}4\underline{0}$ BAMBI
4. $10\underline{5}9\,10\overline{3}\,10\,2\,2\,7$ CINDERELLA
5. $7\,2\overline{7}\overline{9}\overline{9}0\underline{5}$ ALADDIN
6. $4\,10\overline{7}5\overline{2}6\ \ \overline{7}5\underline{9}\ \ \overline{2}8\,10\ \ 4\,10\overline{7}1\overline{2}$ BEAUTY AND THE BEAST
7. $2\overline{7}\underline{9}6\ \ \overline{7}5\underline{9}\ \ \overline{2}8\,10\ \ 2\overline{3}\overline{7}4\underline{9}$ LADY AND THE TRAMP
8. $101\ \ \overline{9}7\underline{2}4\overline{7}\overline{2}0\overline{8}5\overline{1}$ DALMATIONS
9. $\overline{10}7\underline{5}2\overline{7}1\underline{0}7$ FANTASIA
10. $8\,10\overline{3}15\,2\,10\overline{7}$ HERCULES
11. $9\overline{8}17\overline{8}\overline{8}5\overline{2}7\overline{1}$ POCAHONTAS
12. $\overline{2}8\,10\ \ 2\,0\overline{2}\overline{2}2\,10\ \ \overline{4}\,10\overline{3}4\overline{7}0\underline{9}$ THE LITTLE MERMAID
13. $\overline{1}5\overline{8}0\ \ \overline{0}8\,0\overline{2}\,10\ \ \overline{7}5\underline{9}\ \ \overline{1}\,10\overline{7}\,10\overline{5}$ $\underline{9}0\overline{7}3\overline{1}0\overline{1}$ SNOW WHITE AND THE SEVEN DWARFS

Page 87

Final Grades

name _____

The grades are recorded but what are the subjects? Use the code to name the subjects studied.

Report Card

Progress Report ___Gretchen Gale___
Name

Grade 4   Teacher ___Mr. Crayns___

B	⌐◦⌐⌐◦	READING
B	∨⌐◦∙⌐◦⌐	SPELLING
A-	☐☐◦∙⌐∨∏	ENGLISH
A	◦⌐>∏	MATH
A-	∨◦⌐⌐◦ ∨×⌐☐◦∨	SOCIAL STUDIES
A-	∨∟⌐☐☐∟☐	SCIENCE
A	∀◦⌐>⌐◦⌐	WRITING
A	∏☐∙∟>∏	HEALTH

C O D E	A B C / D E F / G H I	J K L / M N O / P Q R	S / T U / V	W X • Y / Z

SAY WHAT?!

Page 88

Bonjour

name _____

World Hello is celebrated each year on November 21. Learn how to say "hello" in several languages by referring to the code in the box below.

CODE	A	B	C	D	E	F	G	H	I	J	K	L	M
	14	15	16	17	18	19	20	21	22	23	24	25	26
	N	O	P	Q	R	S	T	U	V	W	X	Y	Z
	1	2	3	4	5	6	7	8	9	10	11	12	13

Chinese — NIHOW   1-22-21-2-10

German — GUTEN TAG   20-8-7-18-1   7-14-20

Greek — YASOU   12-14-22-6-2-8

Hebrew — SHALOM   6-21-14-25-2-26

Italian — BON GIORNO   15-2-1   20-22-2-5-1-2

Turkish — ALO   14-25-2

Swahili — JAMBO   23-14-26-15-2

Japanese — KONNICHI WA   24-2-1-1-22-16-21-22   10-14

Norwegian — GOD MORGAN   20-2-17   26-2-5-20-14-1

Dutch — GOED DAG   20-2-18-17   17-14-20

Spanish — BUENOS DIAS   15-8-18-1-2-6   17-22-14-6

Swedish — GOD DAG   20-2-17   17-14-20

Czech — DOBRY TUN   17-2-15-5-12   17-18-1

French — BONJOUR   15-2-1-23-2-8-5

THE ARTIFICIAL LANGUAGE CALLED ESPERANTO WAS CREATED BY LUDWIG LAZAR ZAMENHOF, A POLISH OPHTHALMOLOGIST!

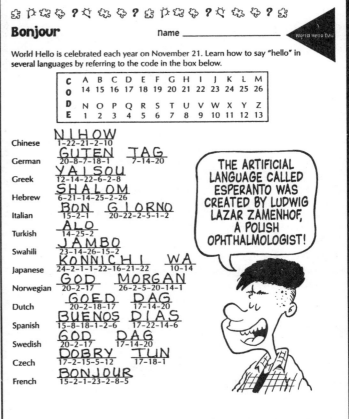

Page 89

The First Holiday

name _____

On November 26, 1789, President George Washington proclaimed Thanksgiving Day as the first United States holiday. Learn the history of this holiday by filling in the blanks with the words from the turkey feathers.

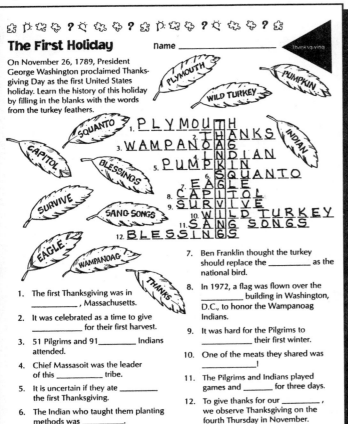

1. P L Y M O U T H
2. T H A N K S
3. W A M P A N O A G
4. I N D I A N
5. P U M P K I N
6. S Q U A N T O
7. E A G L E
8. C A P I T O L
9. S U R V I V E
10. W I L D T U R K E Y
11. S A N G S O N G S
12. B L E S S I N G S

Feathers: PLYMOUTH, PUMPKIN, WILD TURKEY, SQUANTO, INDIAN, CAPITOL, BLESSINGS, SURVIVE, SANG SONGS, EAGLE, WAMPANOAG, THANKS

1. The first Thanksgiving was in _____, Massachusetts.

2. It was celebrated as a time to give _____ for their first harvest.

3. 51 Pilgrims and 91_____ Indians attended.

4. Chief Massasoit was the leader of this _____ tribe.

5. It is uncertain if they ate _____ the first Thanksgiving.

6. The Indian who taught them planting methods was _____.

7. Ben Franklin thought the turkey should replace the _____ as the national bird.

8. In 1972, a flag was flown over the _____ building in Washington, D.C., to honor the Wampanoag Indians.

9. It was hard for the Pilgrims to _____ their first winter.

10. One of the meats they shared was _____.

11. The Pilgrims and Indians played games and _____ for three days.

12. To give thanks for our _____, we observe Thanksgiving on the fourth Thursday in November.

Page 90

"Spare the Acts!"

name _____

Trevor Turkey meant to say "Spare the Ax," but he had homonym trouble. Use colored pencils to underline any incorrectly used homonyms in Trevor's letter. Then write the correct spellings above the homonyms.

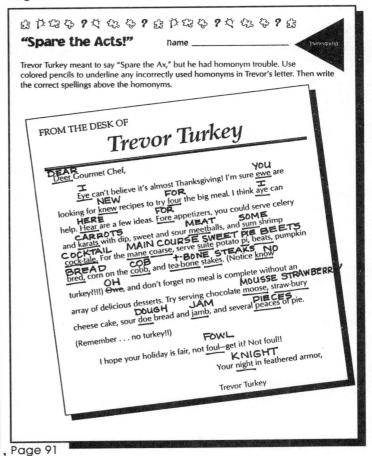

FROM THE DESK OF

Trevor Turkey

DEAR
Deer Gourmet Chef,

I   YOU
Eye can't believe it's almost Thanksgiving! I'm sure ewe are
NEW   FOR   I
looking for knew recipes to try four the big meal. I think aye can
HERE   FOR   MEAT   SOME
help. Hear are a few ideas. Fore appetizers, you could serve celery
CARROTS
and karats with dip, sweet and sour meetballs, and sum shrimp
COCKTAIL   MAIN COURSE SWEET PIE BEETS
cocktale. For the mane coarse, serve suite potato pi, beats, pumpkin
BREAD   COB   +BONE STEAKS NO
bred, corn on the cobb, and tea-bone stakes. (Notice know
OH   MOUSSE STRAWBERRY
turkey?!!!) Owe, and don't forget no meal is complete without an
array of delicious desserts. Try serving chocolate moose, straw-bury
DOUGH   JAM   PIECES
cheese cake, sour doe bread and jamb, and several peaces of pie.

(Remember . . . no turkey!!)
FOWL
I hope your holiday is fair, not foul—get it? Not foul!!
KNIGHT
Your night in feathered armor,

Trevor Turkey

Page 91

On the Right Track

Name _____

Harvey Hunter found these turkey tracks in the woods. Were the turkeys playing jokes on him? Crack the code to find out.

A	B	C	D	E	F	G	H	I	J	K	L	M
●	⌐	✕	▽	⊙	△	⪢	✐	⊡	‖	∧	∧	⪢
N	O	P	Q	R	S	T	U	V	W	X	Y	Z
∨	☀	⊓	⪡	⊔	⊔	♯	⊐	1	★	⌐○	⪡	⫴

1. Why did the hunter only hunt deer? *They were known to bring in* ⌐⊡⪢ ⌐⊐✕∧⊔ __big bucks__

2. What did the hunter call the dried-up river bed? *An* ⊙○♯△●⪢○⪢ __extreme__

3. Why did the hunter think the flowers in the woods were lazy? *They were often found* ⊡∨ ⌐⊙▽⊔ __in beds__

4. What did the hunter call a turkey hit by a bullet? *A* △☀★∧ ⊔✐☀♯ __fowl shot__

5. What did the hunter consider to be the highest form of animal life? *A* ⪢⊡△●△△⊙ __giraffe__

6. What did the hunter call his very own turkey? *A* ⊓⊙△⊔☀∨△ △☀★∧ __personal fowl__

7. How did the hunter define a rooster? *An* ●∧●△⪢ ✕∧⊐✕△ __alarm cluck__

8. What did the hunter call a gun that shoots slow bullets? *A* ⊔∧☀⪢△∨ __slogan__

9. Where was the hunter's favorite stamping ground? *The area around the* ⊓☀⊔♯ ☀△△⊙✕⊙ __post office__

10. Why did the hunter take the deer to the taxidermist? *He really knew* ✐⊡⊔ ⊔♯⊐△△ __his stuff__

Page 92

Where Are We Going?

Name _____

Create a crazy song! Fold this page on the dotted line. While the right side is out of sight, write words in the blanks on the left. Then unfold the page and place your word choices in the song. Sing it to your friends! **ANSWERS WILL VARY.**

1. _____ place
2. _____ celebrity
3. _____ animal
4. _____ verb (present tense)
5. _____ noun
6. _____ verb (present tense)
7. _____ body part
8. _____ body part
9. _____ verb (present tense)
10. _____ animal
11. _____ noun
12. _____ animal
13. _____ verb (present tense)
14. _____ event
15. _____ food
16. _____ dessert

Over the river and through the _____ 1
to _____ 2 's house we go.
The _____ 3 knows the way,
To _____ 4 the sleigh
Through the white and drifted _____ 5 .

Over the river and through the _____ 1
Oh how the wind does _____ 6 .
It stings the _____ 7
And bites the _____ 8
As over the ground we _____ 9 .

Over the river and through the _____ 1
Trot fast, my dapple _____ 10 .
Spring over the _____ 11
Like a hunting _____ 12
For this is Thanksgiving Day.

Over the river and through the _____ 1
Now _____ 2 's cap I _____ 13
Hurrah for the _____ 14 !
Is the _____ 15 done?
Hurrah for the pumpkin _____ 16 !

USE VIVACIOUS VERBAGE!!

Page 93

Ho! Ho! Hoboken!

Name _____

Ho! Ho! Ho!—around the world Santa goes! Discover all the places he'll visit this year. Read the clues and use the Word Box to fill in the letter blanks.

WORD BOX: Hot Springs, Phoenix, Horseshoe Falls, White House, Honduras, Anchorage, Hong Kong, Idaho, Hoboken, Oklahoma, Hoover Dam, Holland, Houston, St. Thomas, Honolulu

1. A New Jersey city on the Hudson River — HO **BOKEN**
2. Alaska's largest city in population — ANC HO **RAGE**
3. The Netherlands — HO **LLAND**
4. Peninsula on the southeast coast of China — HO **NG KONG**
5. Arizona's capital — P HO **ENIX**
6. Central American country — HO **NDURAS**
7. A natural wonder in North America — HO **RSESHOE FALLS**
8. Hawaii's capital — HO **NOLULU**
9. It generates power on the Colorado River — HO **OVER DAM**
10. The president's residence — WHITE HO **USE**
11. The state west of Wyoming — IDA HO
12. City southwest of Little Rock, Arkansa noted for thermal springs — HO **T SPRINGS**
13. Part of the Virgin Islands — ST. T HO **MAS**
14. Home of the Astros — HO **USTON**
15. State north of Texas — OKLA HO **MA**

Page 94

Homonym Hotel

Name _____

The first motel in the United States was opened in December 1925. Read the sentences below. Circle the correct homonym in each sentence and write it in the matching room of the Homonym Hotel.

1 manor	2 Beach	3 Dear	4 Capitol	5 rode	6 Their	7 Meet
8 throne	**9 paced**	**10 knew**	**11 been**	**12 wok**	**13 principal**	

1. We toured an old English (manor, manner).
2. The family went to Virginia (Beech, Beach).
3. The camper's letter began, "(Dear, Deer) Mom and Dad . . ."
4. They visited the (Capital, Capitol) building in Washington, D.C.
5. She (road, rode) the roller coaster four times!
6. (There, their) minivan had a flat tire.
7. (Meet, Meat) me by the diving board at 3:00.
8. The lion king sat on his royal (thrown, throne).
9. The elephants at the zoo (paste, paced) back and forth.
10. We (new, knew) our vacation would be in August.
11. Have you ever (bin, been) to New York City.
12. Our dinner was prepared in a Japanese (walk, wok).
13. Our (principle, principal) vacationed in Florida.

Page 95

Daisy, Daisy . . .

Name _____

Walt Disney's Birthday

December 5 is the anniversary of Walt Disney's birthday. Among his cartoon creations was Daisy Duck. To find out what Daisy Duck's father said to the shop clerk on the day of Daisy's wedding, write each group of words in alphabetical order. Then write the correct words in the matching spaces at the bottom of the page.

A. opossum 1. ON
   once   2. ONCE
   on   3. OPOSSUM
   otter   4. OTTER

B. put   1. PUDDLE
   purse   2. PUMP
   pump   3. PURSE
   puddle   4. PUT

C. mask   1. MARBLE
   myself   2. MASK
   marble   3. MY
   my   4. MYSELF

D. wrong   1. WRAP
   wrap   2. WRIST
   wrote   3. WRONG
   wrist   4. WROTE

E. issue   1. INCH
   it   2. INNOCENT
   inch   3. ISSUE
   innocent 4. IT

F. duty   1. "DUCKS-EDO"
   dusty   2. DUMP
   dump   3. DUSTY
   "ducks-edo" 4. DUTY

G. bird   1. BIGGEST
   binder   2. BILL
   biggest   3. BINDER
   bill   4. BIRD

H. my   1. MY
   money   2. MYLAR
   most   3. MONEY
   Mylar   4. MOST

I. plead   1. PLEA
   plea   2. PLEAD
   please   3. PLEASE
   pleasure 4. PLEASURE

WALT DISNEY WON 30 ACADEMY AWARDS! THAT'S A RECORD!

Answer: PLEASE   WRAP   MY   "DUCKS-EDO" and
         I3   D1   H3   F1
PUT   IT   ON   MY   BILL .
B4   E4   A1   C3   G2

Hot Line to Claus

Name _____

Christmas

1	ABC 2	DEF 3
GHI 4	JKL 5	MNO 6
PRS 7	TUV 8	WXY 9

Claus has a Christmas *challenge* for you. Use the letters on the phone that correspond to the telephone numbers listed below to see what each person might receive for Christmas. You may have to try different combinations. No calling the operator for help!

1. President Clinton (3 words) 263-9729 — a new sax
2. Tiger Woods (2 words) 465-3833 — golf tee
3. R. L. Stein 786-7437 — stories
4. Charles Schultz 732-6887 — Peanuts
5. Garth Brooks 484-8277 — guitars
6. Michael Jordan 763-2537 — sneaker
7. Kristi Yamaguchi (2 words) 423-7465 — ice rink
8. Bugs Bunny 227-7687 — carrots
9. Tony the Tiger 236-3257 — cereals
10. Mickey Mouse (2 words) 244-3277 — big ears
11. Mrs. Claus 266-5437 — cookies
12. Garfield 527-2462 — lasagna
13. The Bulls 842-8679 — victory
14. Sally Ride 227-7853 — capsule
15. Snoopy (2 words) 364-2663 — dog bone
16. Boxcar Children 222-6673 — caboose
17. Pinocchio (2 words) 639-6673 — new nose
18. Dennis the Menace 945-7667 — Wilsons
19. Bill Nye 724-3623 — science
20. Snow White 774-6237 — princes

Candy Canes and Categories

Name _____

Christmas

Santa's shop is a busy place with food, decorations, music, and lots of gift making. Get in the Christmas spirit. Fill in this chart using words that begin with the letters shown at the top of each column. Write as many words as you can for each box. You may use information sources to help your search. Compare your answers with those of two or three classmates, crossing out any that are the same. See which person has the most original items.

POSSIBILITIES INCLUDE

Category	L	I	G	H	T	S
Gift Idea	Lincoln Logs	Ice Skates	Gloves Globe Games Gerbil	Hamster Helicopter	Typewriter Tennis Racket	Skis Sled
Christmas Song Title	Little Drummer Boy	It's Beginning to Look A Lot Like Christmas	God Rest Ye Merry Gentlemen	Hark the Herald Angels Sing	The First Noel	Silent Night Holy Night
Food	Lettuce Lemons Lamb Leeks	Icing Ice-cream	Gravy Grapes Greens Ginger-bread	Honey Ham Hotdog	Turkey Toast	Syrup Sausage Sticky buns
Decorations	Lace Lights Luminaria	Icicles	Garland Glitter Gingham	Halo Holly	Tree Tag Tissue paper	Stocking

---

Habari Gani—What Is the News?

Name _____

Kwanzaa

Kwanzaa is celebrated by African-Americans from December 26 to January 1. The word *Kwanzaa* means first. This holiday is a time to celebrate African-American heritage and ancestral values. Discover more of the tradition of the seven days using the code.

Day 1 ■○□□○ 2 1 2 7 3 UMOJA The day of unity

Day 2 ■□♦♦○■○■□♦○ 7 2 7 1 3 6 3 7 2 1 3 KUJICHAGULIA
The day of self-determination

Day 3 ■□♦○○ 2 7 1 1 3 UJIMA The day of collective work and responsibility

Day 4 ■□○○○○ 2 7 3 1 3 3 UJAMAA The day of cooperative economics

Day 5 ♦♦○ 4 1 3 NIA The day of purpose

Day 6 ■■○□○ 7 2 2 1 6 3 KUUMBA
The day of creativity

Day 7 ♦○○♦ 1 1 3 4 1 IMANI
The day of faith

KWANZAA BEGAN IN 1966!

Traditions include . . .

■○○○○■ 7 3 5 3 1 2
KARAMU , the feast, and

■■○■□○□ 7 1 7 2 1 6 1

♦♦○ ■○□□○ 3 6 3 2 1 2 7 3
KIKOMBE CHA UMOJA ,
the family Kwanzaa cup.

	♦	○	■	□
1	I	M	F	E
2	V	T	U	O
3	C	A	L	W
4	n	Z	Q	D
5	/	R	X	/
6	H	Y	B	S
7	P	G	K	J

© Instructional Fair • TS Denison

IF8727 *Challenge Your Mind*

Nuttin' for Christmas
Name _____ Christmas

Create a crazy song! Fold this page on the dotted line. While the right side is out of sight, write the words in the blanks on the left. Then unfold the page and place your word choices on the appropriate lines in the song. Sing the song to a friend. **ANSWERS WILL VARY.**

1. _____ pair of names
2. _____ classmate
3. _____ verb (past tense)
4. _____ verb (past tense)
5. _____ animal
6. _____ noun
7. _____ body part
8. _____ noun
9. _____ verb (past tense)
10. _____ plural noun
11. _____ plural noun
12. _____ adjective
13. _____ adjective

Chorus
I'm gettin' nuttin' for Christmas, _____1 are mad, I'm gettin' nuttin' for Christmas,
Cause I ain't been nuttin' but bad.
I broke a bat on _____2 's head. Somebody snitched on me.
I _____3 a frog in sister's bed. Somebody snitched on me.
I _____4 some ink on mommy's rug. Somebody snitched on me.
I made _____ eat a _____5
Somebody snitched on me.
I bought some gum with a penny slug. Somebody snitched on me.
Chorus
I put a _____6 on teacher's chair, somebody snitched on me.
I tied a knot in _____ 's _____7, somebody snitched on me.
I did a dance on mommy's _____8 . Somebody snitched on me.
I _____9 a tree and tore my _____10 somebody snitched on me.
I filled the sugar bowl with _____11 . Somebody snitched on me.
Chorus
Next year I'll be _____12 straight,
Next year I'll be good, just wait, I'd start now but it's too
_____13 . Somebody snitched on me.
Chorus

Wreck the Halls?
Name _____ Christmas

Santa's elf, Anthony Antonym, made monstrous mistakes when he posted the Chrismas carol song sheets for this year's festivities. Help him by circling the incorrect word in red or green. Then write the correct antonym on the line. He thanks you "merry, merry much"!

1. (Noisy) Night — **Silent**
2. Oh (Huge) Town of Bethlehem — **Little**
3. (Wreck) the Halls — **Deck**
4. (Black) Christmas — **White**
5. What (Adult) Is This? — **Child**
6. The Twelve (Nights) of Christmas — **Days**
7. (Grouchy) Old Saint Nicholas — **Jolly**
8. (Gloom) to the World — **Joy**
9. Rudolph, the Red (Tailed) Reindeer — **Nosed**
10. (Home) in a Manger — **Away**
11. Santa Claus Is (Going) to Town — **Coming**
12. (Silent) Bells — **Jingle**
13. I'm Getting (Something) for Christmas — **Nuttin'**
14. We Three (Peasants) of Orient Are — **Kings**
15. It Came Upon a Midnight (Smoggy) — **Clear**
16. I Saw (Daddy) Kissing Santa Claus — **Mommy**
17. (Down) on the Housetop — **Up**
18. I'll Be (Gone) for Christmas — **Home**
19. The Little Drummer (Girl) — **Boy**
20. The (Last) Noel — **First**

> THE FIRST CROSSWORD PUZZLE APPEARED IN THE NEW YORK WORLD NEWSPAPER DURING THE CHRISTMAS SEASON OF 1913!

Wise and Witty
Name _____ Poor Richard's Almanac – Published Dec 1732

Benjamin Franklin wrote and published *Poor Richard's Almanac* in December 1732. This book contained proverbs or well-known sayings. Write the letters below in numerical order to complete these proverbs.

1. Early to bed, early to rise, makes a man
   healthy, wealthy and **wise.**
   LYAHHTE TEHLAWY ISEW
   4736 152 52 643 17 2341

2. **Waste** NOT. **Want** NOT.
   ATWES WATN
   24153 1 243

3. If at first you don't **succeed**, try, try **again**.
   CUESCDE GANAI
   3 261475 2 1534

4. You can't **teach** an old **dog** new **tricks.**
   CATEH GD KRCTIS
   4 3125 312 5 24136

5. Better **safe** than **sorry.**
   EFAS YORSR
   4321 5 2314

6. When the **cat's away**, the **mice** will **play.**
   ACTS YAAW ICME YALP
   2134 4132 2314 4321

7. He who **hesitates** is **lost.**
   SETAHITSE TOLS
   327614598 4213

8. One **picture** is worth a **thousand** words.
   CIREPUT HUTODNAS
   3 267154 24 13 8765

9. A **bird** in the **hand** is worth two in the **bush.**
   DIRB DAHN SHUB
   4231 4 213 3421

> BENJAMIN FRANKLIN WAS MADE DEPUTY POSTMASTER GENERAL OF AMERICA IN 1753!

Celebrating Hanukkah
Name _____ Hanukkah

The Jewish holiday Hanukkah begins on the 25th day of the Hebrew month of Kislev. Use the clues and the Word Bank to complete the puzzle.

Across
1. This is what the word Hanukkah means.
2. Homes are decorated in this color and blue, the colors of the Jewish flag.
3. The helper candle (servant) of the menorah.
4. What is given each night of Hanukkah.
5. Candelabra with nine candles.
6. Jews pretended to play with the dreidel when these came near.
7. The dreidel's initials, (nun, gimel, heh, shin) stand for "a great _____ happened there."
8. On Hanukkah, Jewish people give thanks for the _____ of their religion.
9. Hanukkah is also called "_____ of Lights."

Word Bank

dreidel	Hanukkah	nine	gods
rabbi	latkes	temple	Shammash
Judaism	dedication	menorahs	festival
white	gift	miracle	Judah Maccabee
soldiers	survival	Jewish	tradition

Down
1. A Jewish top-like toy
2. _____ families celebrate Hanukkah
3. An inherited custom
4. Festival of Lights
5. Number of candles in a menorah
6. Leader of the Jewish soldiers
7. potato pancakes
8. the Jewish religion
9. They fought against worshiping Greek _____.
10. Jewish house of worship
11. Jewish religious leader

© Instructional Fair • TS Denison

-128-

IF8727 *Challenge Your Mind*